PASSAGES | *Welcome Home to Canada*

MICHELLE BERRY · YING CHEN
BRIAN D. JOHNSON · DANY LAFERRIÈRE
ALBERTO MANGUEL · ANNA PORTER
NINO RICCI · SHYAM SELVADURAI
M.G. VASSANJI · KEN WIWA
MOSES ZNAIMER

Foreword by MICHAEL IGNATIEFF

Preface by RUDYARD GRIFFITHS,
THE DOMINION INSTITUTE

PASSAGES

Welcome Home to Canada

initiated by
WESTWOOD CREATIVE ARTISTS
AND THE DOMINION INSTITUTE

Doubleday Canada

National Library of Canada Cataloguing in Publication Data

Main entry under title:
    Passages : welcome home to Canada.

ISBN 0-385-65893-1

1. Authors, Canadian—20th century—Biography.   2. Immigrants—Canada—
Biography.

PS8081.P39 2002   CD810.9 0054   C2002-903146-X
PR9186.2.P39 2002

Jacket images: *Collage:* GARRY GAY/ THE IMAGE BANK;
    School children (top): COURTESY THE SISTERS OF VIOLA DAVIS DESMOND
Jacket and text design: CS Richardson
Printed and bound in the USA

The contributions of Michelle Berry, Ying Chen, Alberto Manguel, Dany Laferrière,
and Shyam Selvadurai first appeared, in somewhat different form, in *The Globe and Mail.*

Published in Canada by
Doubleday Canada, a division of
Random House of Canada Limited

Visit Random House of Canada Limited's website: www.randomhouse.ca

BVG 10 9 8 7 6 5 4 3 2 1

Contents

Rudyard Griffiths

IMMIGRATION IS THE GREAT Canadian constant. From the first European settlements along the banks of the St. Lawrence, successive waves of immigration have shaped the fabric of Canada. Our political institutions and the importance we put on the values of community and order flow largely from the arrival of the country's first political refugees, the United Empire Loyalists. Canadians' sensitivity to minority rights is an extension of the compromises and complexities of balancing—for the better part of 250 years—the competing interests of French and English, Catholic and Protestant immigrants. In the twentieth century, the movement to create our much-valued social programs such as medicare and social assistance grew out of a Prairie culture shaped in part by Canadians of Eastern European descent.

The interconnections between immigration and the history of Canada are obvious. The fundamental challenge for Canada and Canadians is to see how immigration is shaping our society and values today, and in the future.

We are a country on the verge of transformation, a watershed of not just demographics but of how we think and feel Canadian. In the coming decade, the majority of Canadian citizens will be first- and second-generation immigrants. This majority will consist not of a single mono-cultural group as did, say, the earlier waves of Anglo-European immigration, but of people who have come to Canada from the world over. They will leave jobs, loved ones, and entire cultural frameworks to journey to this county. In Canada, their languages, traditions and values will mix with each other. The only common thread binding these disparate cultures and individuals together will be the experience of being immigrants. At the most basic level, what it means to be Canadian will be an extension of what it means to be an immigrant.

Passages to Canada provides a much-needed window on the contours of this new, radically immigrant identity that is reshaping Canada. While the authors who contributed to this volume come from diverse backgrounds, are at different points in their lives, and express a range of feelings about life in Canada, they share a common mindset. Each has made an epic mental journey. Their respective passages to Canada have made deep impressions on how they think about identity.

As is to be expected, all of the contributors to *Passages to Canada* write powerfully about living with the memories of a lost homeland. Their present-day identities are haunted by the sights and smells of city streets a world away, the caress of a grandfather long dead or the desolation and boredom of a refugee camp. This collection also brings to the fore a sense of the difficulty of integrating into Canadian society. All the contributors feel, at some point in their passage to Canada, the alienation of being an immigrant. Inclement weather, taciturn customs agents or some jarring cultural oddity of Canadian society combine to press on them the identity of an outsider.

Yet it is in this very feeling of otherness that each of the authors finds his or her connection to Canada. By virtue of being an immigrant, they discover in Canada creative freedom and individual autonomy. The broad cultural or deeply personal confines of the identity they left behind in their country of origin have the power of memories only. In Canada they have the ability to construct a sense of self that acknowledges the past but is also open to a present where multiple identities are at play. Being free from a single dominant cultural identity allows them, as writers, to explore and dissect the cultures of their homelands and their adopted country in new and unexpected ways.

Canadian society as a whole needs to be attuned to the question of how to construct, on the model of its recent immigrants, a strong civic identity in a world of rapid change. In the coming decades many of the hallmarks of our identity—medicare, an independent military and even a common border with the United States—will be radically re-worked or abolished. Drawing on the example of recent immigrants, Canadians need to learn to thrive collectively in the absence of a dominant identity based on shared cultural institutions and ethnic memory. And indeed, thanks to how immigrants think and live their multiple identities, Canada shows every indication of sustaining an open, vital and questioning civic culture in an era of intense globalization and value change.

Passages to Canada is much more than a book about immigration. The stories that make up this collection are about universal human truths: the different ways we search for belonging and how we ultimately become reconciled to the lives we create. In final analysis, *Passages to Canada* provides a dose of wisdom that helps us make sense of where we've come from and what we want to accomplish, both as individuals and Canadians.

Michael Ignatieff

INTRODUCTION

WE TEND TO THINK of immigration to Canada as a story of flight from persecution followed by the laying to rest of ancient hatreds. In this scenario, the new land becomes a haven in a heartless world, offering victims escape from mortal danger. *There* was ethnic strife, prejudice and open warfare. *Here* is acceptance. *There* history was a nightmare. *Here* history is a dream of civility. *There* victims endure their history. *Here* victims awaken and begin their history anew. This myth implies that the new land suffers from a deficiency of exciting history. But what native Canadians may live as dullness, our newcomers experience as a welcome deliverance.

This myth of escape has been a pleasant tale to tell, since it presents our country as an island of reason in a sea of fanaticism. This myth also flatters the newcomers, enabling them to present expatriation as an awakening from murderous irrationality.

But was this story ever quite true? Were we ever as welcoming as it makes us out to be? Now that old-world terror has struck at the very heart of the new world, are we quite sure that newcomers are leaving their hatreds behind?

Myths never take hold of the collective imagination if they are pure fantasy. This myth of welcome, together with the myth of hatreds left behind, has just enough truth to be believable. But the writers who've written up their passage to Canada both confirm and challenge these myths. In her account of emigrating from China, Ying Chen tells us that she did indeed find sanctuary here; but she would have us think hard about why Canada, the country of Bethune, should employ officials at its borders who could so frighten and intimidate one of its own citizens. Moses Znaimer, now an irrepressible leader in Canadian broadcasting, escaped the hatreds of his native Europe, but his memoir suggests that no one ever survives hatred unscathed; some people get to safety too late ever to feel quite safe again. He remembers the joylessness and caution of his parents, in their new home in Montreal, and now regards these features as the scars of survival.

The newcomers who here recount their stories are discreet and uncomplaining about the difficulties of becoming a Canadian, but they do suggest that we—Canadians already here—might pay more attention to our myths of welcome. What actually happens in those holding pens in our airports as we sail through the lines reserved for citizens? As a grandson of immigrants myself, I often wonder whether my own people would be able to secure admittance to their grandson's country. In my mind's eye, I see the moment when their miserable sheaf of papers, presented to the government official, comes up short. We have a lot invested in our complacent myths of welcome. Perhaps we should care a little about whether they are still true, or ever were.

Shyam Selvadurai's memoir, with its evocation of the murderous attacks on Tamils in the Sri Lanka of the 1980s, brings into focus the issue of hatred. What happens to inherited hatreds when you pass into exile and emigration? Do they, as our myths would have us believe, wither away in the fresh northern air? There is no hatred in Shyam's memoir—indeed the opposite—but the fact is, there is surpassing hatred in some sections of the Tamil community in Canada.

I remember mourning, in 1999, the passing of Neelan Tiruchelvan, a moderate Tamil friend, who was blown to pieces by a car bomb in Colombo by an extremist Tamil group. His offence? Seeking a peaceful solution to the Sri Lankan catastrophe through negotiations with the Singhala government. After I went to Colombo to mourn his passing and to denounce the act of terror that had claimed his life, I began receiving literature justifying his murder. Well-produced, articulate monthly magazines argued that anyone from the Tamil community who sought non-violent solutions to political problems was either a stooge or a fool, or a little of both. The rhetoric employed was a version of what the French call *la politique du pire:* endorsing strategies to make things worse so that they cannot possibly get better. These Tamil magazines did not actively endorse my friend's death—he was dead already—but they were astonishingly indifferent to it, as if the undoubted sufferings of the Tamil people justified the abrogation of the simplest expressions of human pity. His body, after all, had been cut to pieces, and his life, a monument to political reason, had been cut short. I left off reading these documents with the sense that I had nothing to say to the people who had written them. The point of this story is that these magazines had been sent to me from a Canadian city. They had actually been printed and published on my native soil.

The episode made me rethink our myth about the passage to Canada as being from hatred to civility. Was it true now? Was it ever true? As I recalled my Canadian history, I began to question this myth that the passage to Canada was a gentle forgetting of inherited political anger. The Irish carried their hatreds among their meagre belongings on the emigrant ships of the 1840s, and the visceral dislike of Orangeman for Fenian was a defining feature of Ontario politics from then until the 1890s. The vast Slavic and southern European migrations of Laurier's Canada also transported their political grievances here. Emigrants from the Balkans did not forget or forgive the oppression that had caused them to flee. Did Canadian Serbs rejoice at the assassination of Franz Ferdinand in Sarajevo in June 1914? It's hard to imagine that most did not, since this act of terror was held to herald the liberation of Bosnia from Austro-Hungarian rule. Yet Serbs and non-Serbs alike quickly learned that terror can have consequences as catastrophic as they are unforeseen—in this case, a world war that would last four years and claim some 20 million lives.

In the next great wave of Canadian immigration, beginning after World War II, migrants from

Czechoslovakia, Poland, the Baltic States and other territories under Soviet tyranny came to this country with all their hatreds intact. Let us not suppose that hatred is necessarily a bad thing: sometimes it is good to hate oppression, and the Canadians who, whenever the Bolshoi Ballet toured Canada, held up signs outside the theatre protesting Soviet tyranny now seem more prescient and morally aware than those, and they included myself, who thought it was time to acquiesce to the facts of life, i.e. the permanent Soviet occupation of Eastern Europe. In particular, the Baltic families who maintained their opposition to Soviet tyranny while in Canada throughout the long Cold War then lived to see their sons and daughters return, after 1991, to a free Estonia, Latvia and Lithuania. Here, political hatred—or at least loathing of despotism—was sustained, not forgotten, in the passage to Canada, and since in this case hatred did not also incubate or support acts of terror, it seems to have been a positive thing. It is not always right for exile and emigration to be accompanied by political forgetting. Remembering a conquered or oppressed home is one of the duties of those who escape to a better life.

The problem is that exile can freeze memory and conviction at the moment of departure. Once abroad, groups often fail to evolve or change their thinking. And when they return, once their country is free, they speak and behave as if it were still 1945. A case in point would be Croatian exiles who fled to Canada in the 1940s to escape Tito's imposition of Communist rule over Yugoslavia. In exile, they remained more nationalistic than would have been allowed in Tito's postwar Croatia. Preserving a nation's pride is one thing; allowing it to congeal in forgetful myth is another. It is difficult enough for any people to face the historical truth about their country, and this becomes almost impossible when they also lose that country. Such might have been the dilemma for young Canadian Croatians who went into exile after 1945. Having lost their country, how could they bear to admit that Ante Pavelic's wartime regime had been responsible for atrocities against Jews, Serbs, Roma and other minorities? Facing up to the reality of Pavelic's regime could not have been easy in Zagreb. It turned out to be just as difficult in Toronto. Indeed, it was often said in Zagreb that the chief support for the most intransigent and aggressive nationalism in Croatia after independence in 1991 was to be found not in Zagreb, but in Toronto.

Canadians born here tend to be indifferent to or ignorant of the dual political allegiances of many of their fellow citizens from diasporic communities. Yet these diasporas may be loyal to Canadian institutions and at the same time be in violent opposition to the political system they have left behind. These dual allegiances are complex: a recently minted citizen who would not think of assassinating a fellow Canadian from some oppressor group does not hesitate to fund assassinations of the same group in another country. Sometimes emigration is accompanied by guilt, and this can make diasporic groups more violent and extreme than those who live in the country where the oppression is taking place. The difficult truth—which makes diasporic nationalism a dangerous phenomenon—is that it is easier to hate from a distance. You don't have to live with the consequences—or the reprisals.

Canadians, new and old, need to think about what role their diasporas play in fanning and financing the violent hatreds of the outside world. Our comfortable myth is that our country serves as a refuge for people seeking to escape hatred. The more disturbing reality is that some of our diasporas actively support and encourage violence. Are we so sure that acts of terror in Kashmir do not originate in apparently innocent donations to charitable and philanthropic appeals in Canadian cities? Are we certain that the financing of a car bomb in Jerusalem did not begin in a Canadian community? Do we know that when people die in Colombo—or for that matter in Jaffna—there is not a Canadian connection?

I do not have answers to these questions, and it would be fatuous, not to mention inflammatory, to point fingers without evidence. My point is not to make allegations but to ask us to rethink our myths of immigration, particularly that innocent one that portrays us as a haven from a heartless world, a refuge from hatred. It is clear to me that this was never entirely true: many of the immigrant groups who have made their lives here began not by extinguishing but by fanning the hatreds they brought with them. If it has always been true that most immigrant groups arrive in this country with some considered detestation of the oppressors who drove them out of their homeland in the first place, it would be invidious and inconsistent to single out any particular group arriving now for particular condemnation or investigation.

We are naïve if we assume that immigration ever meant assimilation in the strict sense of discarding identity. New identities never obliterate old ones, and new identities are unlikely to be authentic and strong if they are built on forgetting. Moreover, to ask new

Canadians to forget old selves would be to squander their unique contributions to their adopted country. The most useful new Canadians are those who have refused to think of their passage to Canada as a process of discarding.

For example, anyone who has heard the writer and translator Alberto Manguel speak would find it hard to place his accent. This marvellous Canadian writer speaks and writes an English flavoured with Spanish and French, and heaven knows what else besides. One key to his creativity, it would seem, is his refusal to give up anything, his refusal to allow the passage to Canada to repress a single feature of a highly complex, multi-dimensional identity. Anna Porter, a Canadian publisher, a Hungarian New Zealander, has done more than most native-born Canadians to promote the literature of her adopted home, but her residual identities have never been renounced, and indeed have become stronger as she became a Canadian. She remains the Hungarian émigré of the 1956 era, whose Budapest grandfather was a publisher. Her life in Canada represents a keeping of faith with his inspiration.

And after all, as these memoirs assure us, the Canadian immigration myth is sometimes quite accurate. This might be so in the case of the son of

Ken Saro-Wiwa, the martyred leader of the Ogoni
people of Nigeria. Being the son of a hero and a
martyr is to live under a light-obliterating shadow.
In Canada, it seems, the son has not so much
thrown off the shadow of the father as found the
distance to live under it in peace with himself. In
other cases, emigration allows newcomers to find
identities that were not permitted or not even per-
ceived in the past. For Shyam Selvadurai, coming to
Canada created the possibility of finding a sexual
identity that had not been possible in Sri Lanka.
The message of these memoirs is that migrants love
a new country to the degree that it allows them to
be free, to keep the identities they cherish and to
fashion ones anew.

Nevertheless, it would be a good idea, once and
for all, to get a few things clear. Canada means many
things to many people—and in the debate about
what it means, new voices are as valuable as older
ones—but one thing is indisputable: we are a political community that has outlawed the practice or
advocacy of violence as an instrument of political
expression. We have outlawed it within, and we
need to outlaw it without. Just as we have laws
against racial incitement or the promulgation of ethnic hatred, in order to protect our new citizens from

bigotry, abuse and violence, so we must have laws that allow for the prosecution of anyone in Canada who aids, abets, encourages or incites acts of terror. There may be political causes that justify armed resistance, but there are none that justify the terrorization and murder of civilians. The distinction between freedom fighters and terrorists is not the relativist quagmire we are led to suppose it is. There are laws of war governing armed resistance to oppression, just as there are laws of war governing the conduct of hostilities between states. Those who break these laws are barbarians, whatever the cause they serve. Those who target civilians to cause death and create fear are terrorists, no matter how justified their cause may be. States that use terror against civilians are as culpable as armed insurgents.

Coming to Canada is not the passage from hatred to civility that we innocently suppose it to be. It never has been. Frankly, some hatreds—of oppression, cruelty, racial discrimination—will be wanted on the voyage, and will be kept on our soil. There is nothing Canadian society can or should do about this. But Canada can keep to one simple rule of the road: we are not a political community that aids, abets, harbours or cultivates terror. So it is appropriate to say the following to newcomers: You do not have to embrace all our supposed civilities. You do not have to assimilate to our forms of innocence. You can and should keep the memory of the injustice you have left behind firmly in your heart. But the law is the law. You will have to leave your fantasies of revenge behind.

———

$\mathcal{M.G.}$ Vassanji

CANADA AND ME:
FINDING OURSELVES

I FIRST CAME TO CANADA as a postdoctoral fellow at the nuclear laboratory in Chalk River, Ontario. Having come from the United States and lived all my life in urban centres, I was quite under the impression that I had struck out far north into the woods. It was August and, as if to confirm my impression, the leaves were already beginning to turn yellow. On the way in from Montreal, the towns we passed looked small and laid back, and the people, when we had to stop, seemed grimly reserved compared with the Americans I had known. I felt apprehensive but venturesome, with all the cockiness of the city dweller. On my first day at work, when I was asked how I found my new surroundings, I answered that I felt a bit like David Livingstone, meaning, like a foreigner among natives in a far-off jungle place. I don't know what shocked my hosts more, my estimation of the place or my inversion of the role of the native. It's not so bad, said one of them, red-faced, a British-born scientist.

And it wasn't so bad, after all. In my new surroundings I learned to find pleasure in solitude and
in the textures and colours of the forest; and although
I couldn't quite get a glow of emotion going at the
sight of a flock of migrating geese in the fall and
spring, or feel that twinge of hardy satisfaction
whenever the minimum temperature had hit the
legendary minus forty the previous night, I did learn
to appreciate the sky and watch the stars. My neigh-
bour was an amateur astronomer who most evenings
took out his telescope into the backyard and turned
it skywards. I did my watching by myself though,
on dark clear nights, walking along the inky black
Ottawa River, wondering about the lights that
glowed so enigmatically through the windows of the
toylike bungalows on the silent, empty streets, and
always aware of the moon, if there was one, making
its slow descent on the other side of the water, where
lay the province of Quebec. I learned cross-country
skiing in a town whose inhabitants sometimes skied
ten miles to work, and one of whom actually cycled
there in all seasons. During my second time out on
the cross-country trails, when I had not slipped and
fallen as many times as on the previous occasion,
I walked back home with my skis on my shoulders

and, tropical boy that I was, removed my hat because I was feeling hot. The result was a crisp glazing of ice on my stinging red ears when I returned to my apartment.

Rents were cheap. Whereas I had lived in single rooms and studios the past eight years as a student, now I had a bright and roomy two-bedroom apartment all my own to walk around in. I read Pascal with my morning coffee. I did not have a television and patiently translated from medieval Gujarati texts during my spare time, and I began my first novel, of which I never finished more than the first two chapters. I suspect that my most recent novel was the final manifestation of that early attempt, which had been too close to my recent personal experiences as a student in the United States.

Deep River, the town where I lived, had a population of 5500 and was actually not more than three hours east on the highway from Ottawa; obviously it was far from the northern outpost I had imagined it to be. To qualify for my luxurious (as it seemed then) furnished apartment, company rules demanded that I be married. I had a fiancée in Boston and we had planned to marry the following year. For the sake of the apartment, my fiancée—who had come with a couple of friends to drop me off at this northern frontier—and I decided it would not be a bad idea to marry, if only formally. So we went knocking at the house of the local Lutheran pastor. As a student I had gained the impression that Lutherans were liberal; their pastor at my university had been a woman. This one was a large, chubby man, and he agreed to marry two non-Christians the next day in church, with our two friends from Boston as witnesses. His wife, though, wore a severe suspicious look right from the moment we stepped out of that small, modern church. We did feel a little guilty, but we also respected the blessing we had received. The real, traditional wedding took place some eight months later.

Civilization for me meant Montreal, where I had some friends, and where my wife would come from Boston to meet me every few weeks. The bus back from Montreal left at nine P.M. on Sunday night, and I remember being amazed at the tearful partings of passengers who were going only as far as North Bay or Sudbury. The bus would drop me on the highway, in the still of the northern night, and I would walk my lonely way home on the main road into town. Once, I was followed all the way by a fox trotting along a ditch by the road; another time, the local police cruiser gave me a ride. And I recall, too, standing at the side of the highway at two-thirty A.M.

waiting for the bus to drop off my beloved, tired and sleepy, but undoubtedly happy.

Two years after my arrival, when my fellowship ended, I departed for Toronto, but not without a touch of sadness. I could not have spent the rest of my life in such a small and faraway place; nevertheless, I would miss this one. I did return to visit it a few times. Once while driving back, we had to stop for a couple of black bears in the middle of Algonquin Park. Now, I had seen elephants in the wild, and the sight of giraffe, zebra, and wildebeeste was routine fare on a road trip between Kenya and Tanzania. Still, those bears and that drive through Algonquin remain memorable. As memorable, and a bit embarrassing, was the occasion when a family of raccoons passed us late one night as we sat by a fire outside a cabin we had rented. We were so frightened, unused to these strange nocturnal animals, that they might well have been a pride of lions in the Serengeti.

Since those first years I have travelled from coast to coast in this country, from sea to shining sea, and by land as well as by air. My family and I have driven to the Maritimes several times, via Quebec City (where, much to our amazement, the Plains of Abraham were not as spectacular as we had expected but where we discovered an Indian restaurant worth making a special trip for), and toured the charming picture-postcard coastlines of New Brunswick and Nova Scotia. We have travelled by train to Vancouver, across northwestern Ontario (disappointingly scrubby), the endlessly flat Prairies that could mesmerize, and the simply spectacular Rockies. With Montreal we have a special relationship; it was the first Canadian city I ever saw, when as a student in Boston I bagged a ride to go there just for the heck of it. It was where my wife and I would arrange to meet, where I went to see civilization, as I called it. And so I believe I have seen the country as few Canadians have.

The foregoing is surely a satisfying immigrant story, especially if I conclude it with my subsequent career.

And yet. And yet, something else, someplace else never ceases to beckon, to claim a place in my heart. I am a two-timer.

When I hear the national anthem of Canada or even of the United States, I cannot resist the refrain tugging at my mind of *Mungu ibariki Afrika*, the first lines of the Tanzanian anthem, "God bless Africa." This is not an affectation; I do not consciously dredge it up. It is a part of my being. It is a tic, it is unconscious, it is a love. I remain strongly attached to Africa, the continent of my birth; its music, the sight of its grasslands, its red earth, or its mighty Kilimanjaro, stir me to the core. I have happy memories of my childhood there.

Is there something wrong with me? Am I a traitor? A wretched ingrate? Don't I know that I am privileged to live in "the best country in the world"? Shouldn't I be thankful for my freedoms, my high standard of living, my relative safety? Have I forgotten how I left my country—by stealth—and that I remained afraid for two decades to visit it? Hasn't my adopted country Canada lavished generosity and recognition upon me?

There is some risk in what I write; for I have been invited as a Canadian writer to contribute to these pages, Canadian readers expect something from me, and they have a right to. They have been generous and given me a literary home. My work would have been an orphan without this country. But I believe for that very reason it behooves me to be absolutely honest, to bare my heart to them. We live currently in flag-draping times, as I see them, in which the flag is often the resort of the rogue and the huckster, to paraphrase Samuel Johnson. The red-and-white banner is used to sell anything from beer to sports clothing, politicians to news broadcasts, and historical, not to say moral, objectivity is often swept aside by the jingoism it has come to represent. This loud nationalism, like the ready applause of some-one who always jumps to his feet at a concert, puts in a difficult position those who would show their appreciation more quietly and perhaps with a more complex mix of feelings. I believe what I want to say is neither dishonest, nor treacherous, nor unpatriotic.

I am not afflicted by nostalgia. I have visited the land of my birth many times and have no illusion that it remains what it was in the past. The population has increased four times or more since I lived there, resulting in large unemployment; my family and a good part of the Indian community within which I grew up have emigrated; there are new ways of thinking, particularly an endemic dependence on foreign "donors," that are reprehensible to me, brought up as I was on the concepts of self-help and dignity; foreign city-planners without adequate knowledge of my former city's history or peoples have played havoc with its neighbourhoods. But it is still a place that feels, to some degree, like home. It is possible for me to pass for a local, raising no suspicions of a life overseas. And its pain is to some degree my pain.

A girl from Uganda writes to me (having received the impression from somewhere that I am a big philanthropist): I am eighteen years old, my younger brother and sister and I are orphans, our parents died of AIDS; please send me some money to finish college. Another one writes: My village in northern Uganda was raided, my family was killed and I was abducted. I have managed to reach Kampala and need money to finish high school. There is no easy way to authenticate these stories, even if I could afford to send thousands of dollars.

What does it mean to be a Canadian? What does it mean for me to be anybody in the world? I have often been plagued by these questions of identity. I feel guilty—first, for not being an unequivocal Canadian, and for the impressions I must be passing on to my Toronto-born kids; and second, for living in relative affluence, worrying about material comforts in a land glutted upon them, spoiling those same kids silly, when the land that gave me birth and some of my happiest memories lives in such anguish of war, crime, corruption, deprivation. There are, of course, ways of giving back, of making a contribution. What I am describing, however, is a state of being, the guilt of the one who got away, the guilt of the survivor, if you will.

When I was a teenager, we were taught a lesson in responsibility that I have never been able to forget. One child out of twenty, we were told, had the privilege of reaching high school; and the child who gets to high school and university is like the boy or girl who is fed all the food in a starving village so that he or she can reach the next village to bring back help for all. I was one of those children. And in my absence, further havoc has been wreaked on that village.

Am I doomed to a state of in-betweenness? Is it really a doom? Is it time to stop fooling ourselves and admit that I am a Canadian citizen, with loyalties and attachments in the country, but essentially—because I have attachments elsewhere—a homeless person?

How easy it seems to say that I am a Canadian, that nothing else matters; history began the day I obtained my immigrant status, and the past before that has been totally obliterated. If I say that loud enough I might even be called upon to promote beer. But my affliction is history, memory. It is history and memory that living in Toronto has nurtured to inspire the novels and stories I write. And, ironically, it is a history and memory of a nomad life and constant exile.

I am an East African Canadian of Indian origin. I have also called myself an African Asian Canadian. I was born in Nairobi, Kenya, and brought up in Dar es Salaam, Tanzania. My mother's parents were born in India and emigrated to East Africa, at a time when both those regions of the world were part of the British Empire. My paternal grandfather was born in

Kenya and therefore I have come to believe, with a
certainty that however is not absolute, that his father
must have migrated to Africa in the 1880s. My great-
grandmother most likely came with him. My own
parents never saw India.

There is an interesting, rather touching story
about my father as a restless young man. Apparently
he once stowed away on a steamer bound from
Mombasa to the ancestral homeland. There were several such ships that went to India, and as children we
knew them all by name: SS *Kampala,* SS *Karanja,*
SS *Amra,* SS *Bombay.* But my father, when his ship
reached Bombay, wasn't allowed to disembark
because he had no papers. I have always imagined him
viewing glittering, legendary Bombay, the city of film
stars, through steamer portholes. The story, partly
apocryphal perhaps, symbolizes for me the status of
my family and of many others like them. It represents
the eternal quest for a home, and its constant denial.

My father was a wanderer in East Africa, I've
learned, until he married my mother and settled
down. My mother was born on the island of Zanzibar,
then brought to Mombasa, where she grew up. She
was married in Nairobi to my somewhat vagabond of
a father, an orphan of good family; when he died, my
mother took us all to Dar es Salaam, where her family

had moved. Later she moved back to Nairobi, and later still to Syracuse, New York, with my younger brother, whence to Calgary, Alberta.

And so wanderlust is a part of my heritage, as is the quest for home. With every departure comes a sense of loss, of something left behind; and if you are a novelist, you find yourself out on that quest for comprehensibility, for the beginning of history and the sources of memory, not just your own and your family's, but also communal history and memory. History, slipping away like grains of sand through the fingers, becomes obsession. Because, although there is no denying the gains brought about by emigration, with each move—from India to Africa, within Africa, from Africa to North America—we fragmented our stories, lost parts of our history, and carried the broken-up remains like a peddler's items in a sack.

A few years ago, at a gathering in film director Deepa Mehta's house in Toronto, I met a rather dapperly dressed man with the surname Fancy. I was pleasantly surprised to encounter him. We had never met before, but I had heard of his family. The Fancys were a prominent family of Pakistan known by name even in East Africa. I told Mr. Fancy that my mother said we were related on my father's side to the Fancys. As a child I had not paid much attention to such stories;

who were the Fancys of Pakistan to us in Dar? This
Mr. Fancy, though, said yes, he knew we were related.
He had apparently heard of me. He told me that my
grandfather, who had died young, had had two brothers. One of them went to live in Mwanza, a town on the
shore of Lake Victoria. There, he happened to be in
court once, wearing a suit and hat, and drew the attention of the British judge, who commended him on his
fancy attire. He immediately adopted the name Fancy.
He later went to Pakistan, and was the grandfather of
the friendly gentleman before me, my distant cousin.

And so, reacquaintance with a lost branch of the
family, a story from the past, even an acquaintance
with a clan name (which he told me was Bhimani)
that we had lost due to my father's early death and the
subsequent loss of contact with his side of the family.

As a young man at university I searched anxiously
and deeply for my real identity, some essence that
defined me. Was I Indian or African? Both identities
were under threat by my presence in North America.
Although I had come to the United States to attend
university, the trend was for young people like me not
to return. Still, Africa, Tanzania, meant a lot to me. In
Boston, whenever some Indian student would accost
me (this was not unusual at the time) with, Are you
from India? I would proudly say I was from Tanzania.

Some of the Indians would then persist: Yes, but originally from where?

Of course they were right. I was also in some way an Indian. But in what way? I painstakingly studied Indian culture, history and philosophy, struggling in vain to find my exact place in that vast, incomprehensible matrix whence I had emerged. I came across moments of self-discovery in the films of Satyajit Ray, in the Bengali language I did not understand, that astounded me. I also studied with fascination the history of East Africa, devoured accounts written by the European explorers and administrators, their descriptions of the Indian traders they came across, among whom were my Gujarati ancestors.

At the same time that I was consumed by this search for identity, my stay in the United States was altering me, westernizing me in indelible ways. For one thing, although I had been brought up in a very religious community, no longer could I define myself solely by religious faith, which for me had become a matter of personal philosophy and belief. This fact is brought home to me every time I travel east.

I now have realized that what I am is simply the sum of what has gone into me. I am happy to live with several identities and with the contradictions that that implies; in fact I thrive on them, they feed my creativity. The ultimate wisdom, the secret of my life, is that there is no resolution, no real, single essence of me. This sounds a bit like Zen self-discovery perhaps, and trivial maybe, but it is of profound consequence for me personally. The difference from that other kind of enlightenment is that it produces no calm ocean of wisdom in my mind, no unifying tranquility, but instead a field of felt tensions that defines me.

I even realized recently that my sin of heresy—equivocation—my claim to many identities may have deeper roots. The migration of my family, that itch in the foot, did not start with the generation that left a drought-ridden western India taking to the dhows to cross the Indian Ocean for the greener pastures of Zanzibar and East Africa. There also was an earlier, and incomplete, migration of the psyche. That migration was the conversion of my people from a Hindu sect into a sect of Islam. We were a syncretistic community, sometimes considered heretical, who saw nothing wrong and felt no qualms in subscribing to beliefs from both faiths. We couldn't, did not want to, let go.

Africa is my history and my memory. It is inside me. And so is India, in its way, though I do not wish to bring in that further complication here.

One is sometimes taunted, Then why did you come here? The question is both naïve and presumptuous. A serious, existential question about the here and now is not answered by, Then why did you come? The undeniable fact is, I have come and here I am. Three hundred thousand immigrants come to Canada every year, to keep this nation viable. The world has changed. Population growth statistics for the Western countries indicate that they can continue to thrive only with the influx of immigrants. The populations of African and Asian countries, on the other hand, are exploding. It takes no clever guessing to tell where some of these extra populations will end up. And it is important for this to be the case if our planet is to keep conflicts between rich and poor to a minimum. Surely the nature of the world's developed nations, especially those that must depend on immigrants, must change.

I recall how, in the 1960s, when Kenyan Asians with British passports started going to England to claim their residency rights there, they were faced with vicious public protests. Enoch Powell, eminent classical scholar and Conservative politician, announced famously, by way of protest, that England is fish and chips, not rice and curry. Forty years later now, rice and curry is precisely one of the items Britain

promotes in its self-image. And only recently it allo-
cated permits to Indian teachers to go there and teach.
What was unthinkable once sounds natural now.

It is cometimes argued that Canada needs a strong
identity, a sense of its essential self and destiny, such
as the United States possesses. An American does not
feel two ways about being American. If immigrants
are allowed to live in Canada without coelescing or
assimilating into an unequivocal national identity,
goes this argument, they will only contribute further
to this country's character as a confused, hapless
nonentity on the world stage.

But America is the wrong model. It is an older,
more established, more populous country, which
came into being with a strong founding mythology
and began with a war of revolution. American identity is a religion; in that it is surely unique. Watching
the American flag ceremony at an event such as the
Super Bowl, pitched with emotion and fervor, is as
wonderful and mysterious and awesome as seeing a
few thousand Muslims kneeling in solemn prayer,
turned towards Mecca, or conservative Jews at the
Wailing Wall.

Canada is where the Loyalists came. It was part of
the British Empire, which is why people from the former British colonies found it easier to come to it.

With a larger percentage of new immigrants, it presents a lesser inertia to change. It welcomes and accommodates the world, and as a result it reflects global diversity in a peaceful mode. That should surely be its strength and its identity, its uniqueness—not its source of insecurity.

The destruction of the World Trade Center brought home dramatically, to many of us in Canada, how tenuous is the concept of a narrow, inflexible national identity. In the days and weeks that followed September 11, there were many cries of, "We are all Americans." Canada ran out of American flags. The rallying cry had always been, "We are *different* from Americans." The more nationalist-minded Canadians used to bristle with anti-Americanism. The difference between the two nations was something which many immigrants, who had seen Canada as merely an extension of America from afar, had to learn, much to their embarrassment and the consternation of those who reminded them of this.

So what happened? September 11 showed that there are ties that are impossible to forget or break. They may be historic, they may be racial, tribal or geographic, but they are there in the mind. And when the world, among commentators and analysts, began to be divided among "us" and "them," or the

"Roman Empire" and the "Barbarians," or clashing civilizations, then, however we interpret these concepts (and they are fundamentally contestable), it was clear that the time of narrow nationalism was over in more ways than one.

And if we were all Americans at that particular crisis moment, and perhaps are still if we view the crisis as long-term and global, then is it asking too much for us to be Africans too, when that continent is in crisis? Or Indians or Chinese, if the occasion demands? Is it so morally reprehensible or unpatriotic to be aware of all one's origins and therefore care about a larger world, to care especially about the poorer segments of the globe, whence one has come, and to which one has not repaid any debt?

That, ultimately, is my defence, my plea for redemption. I have justified my equivocation, my heresy, by saying that it is natural and inevitable in the modern world, which is so interconnected and so fraught with dangers that arise from differences among peoples. The justification is what I have arrived at, but the sin is a matter of the heart, is what I am.

✒️ Manguel

DESTINATION ITHACA

THE TROGLODYTES WHO, along with the mammoth and the sabre-toothed tiger, wandered into Russia across the Bering Strait; the ancient South Americans who (according to Thor Heyerdahl) arrived on the rocks of Easter Island and mysteriously erected the colossal faces of their abandoned gods; the Italian boy from Edmundo d'Amici's *Cuore* who travelled from the Apennines to the Andes in search of his long-lost mother; the Jews who crossed the desert, following a column of dust by day and a column of fire by night; Aeneas who, with his father on his back, blindly sought to found the birthplace of the poet who would one day make him immortal; General Lavalle's soldiers, who carried the rotting corpse of their heroic leader from the mountainous North to the plains of Buenos Aires, during the Wars of Independence; Nemo, who bore his anger twenty thousand leagues beneath the seven seas; Candide on his long peregrinations whose goal (he doesn't know this) is a garden; Monkey, Horse and Pig, who walked westwards to India in search of the sacred books; Eric the Red, who discovered America too early for the constraints of history; the brother and sister who left their house to find the elusive Blue Bird—all my childhood long, I was haunted by wanderers and their migrations. My books were full of them.

They fascinated me, these departures, partly because every excursion promised a flight from the confines of my days, and partly because the outcome of the adventure was somehow still in the future, where everything was possible. It seemed to me that no arrival was the true end of the story: Gulliver set off again after having returned from his travels, and Alice, after waking, passed her dream on to her sister, whose dreamer she had become. Something in the very roundness of the world suggests that every journey is always to be continued.

Even though I grew up travelling, the wisdom around me told me that I should stand still in one place. *"Kosmopolitt!"* spat out my grandmother, to insult a distant cousin who had never sprung roots in any of the cities in which he had lived. *"A Man Should Only Eat Bread from Wheat Grown on His Native Land"* was the title of one of the texts in my grade four reading book (this in Argentina, a country made up of immigrants). And our national epic, the *Martín Fierro*, gave as advice to its readers: "Stick to the little corner / Where you first came to this earth. / A cow that keeps changing pastures / Will be late in giving birth." But what was that corner where I first came to this earth? My passport said "Buenos Aires"; in my dreams I was not so certain.

My earliest memories are of a wild park of sandy dunes where bushes of pink and white flowers gave off a sickly smell, and where giant tortoises made their slow way to the hot sea beyond. Also: a garden with four tall palm trees carrying bunches of deep yellow nuts; a cool, dark basement nursery with stuffed animals and many books; a large white kitchen where the cook would give me chunks of cheese and baking chocolate.

My memories are memories of memories; repetition has sorted them out, chronologically, and dusted off the cobwebs. Now I remember an excursion to the salt mines of Sodom, where the walls looked like the inside of an icebox dripping frozen tears; a huge canvas depicting a sea battle on the wall of a Venice palazzo that reeked of honeyed wax; the donkey ride in the Luxembourg Gardens, while loud birds sang in the trees; a train stopping at a small German station and a gift of tiny wooden animals painted in fierce bright colours; a walk up a mountain path following the Stations of the Cross and being told the story of Christ as if it were another of my gory fairy tales. Images of Buenos Aires are from much later, and lack the same intensity in colour, smell and sound; they begin when I was seven and my family had returned to the city. But by then I was conscious of remembering.

In order to migrate to a certain place, you must leave another. This truism is not as simple as it seems. Nothing tells you at what precise point departure ends and arrival begins; what goodbyes are forever, what street signs you are seeing for the last time, what doors you have locked behind you and will never open again. Once your back is turned, the landscape shifts, objects lose their shape, people take on other voices and other faces. In your presence, all change is gradual, almost imperceptible, as the minutes gnaw at the hours; the colours fade, the sounds grow fainter, so that the transformation itself becomes a familiar process. But in your absence, change is vertiginous. You believe you hold a place in your memory, fast and immutable, like those miniature scenes under a plastic dome where nothing but the weather changes with a brisk shake of your hand; but the very instant the place is out of your sight it is no longer yours, the way you knew it. The place you think you remember melts and shimmers in your mind's eye, like the ruins of a city on the bottom of a lake; while back where you left it the place grows, flourishes, sprouts feathers or tentacles, becomes unrecognizable. So while you think, with more or less certainty, that you are leaving a place, the place is leaving you too, receding into itself, drifting away from you, irretrievably, decisively, unfaithful at the very moment of farewell, long before you have admitted to yourself that this time, maybe, it is forever. You have not quite left, but you are no longer there where you once were, in that place you thought of as home. The place itself is now another.

I remember the shock of realizing, when I returned for a short spell to Buenos Aires a few years after leaving in the late sixties, that the house to which we had moved when I was seven, in which I had grown up while attending school for eleven years, where I had spent my entire adolescence and had celebrated my twentieth birthday, that this house had been torn down and nothing, not a trace of it remained. The cobbled street along which the soda-water vendor would rattle his horse-drawn cart, laden with blue and green glass siphons that glittered like ornaments on a Christmas tree, had been covered with smooth asphalt; the corner building, which was the signpost signalling arrival after the long bus ride home, had been turned into bleak offices; the pharmacy across from us, where a gargantuan nurse once stitched my knee after a nasty fall, had disappeared; the small bookstore down the way which sold the novels of Jules Verne in bright yellow covers, and notebooks in which I once wrote grandiose epic poems and tragic plays, was no longer there. I had been gone for only three or four years, barely long enough to wonder if I would ever return, and already everything was different, alien, meaningless, so that the question of coming back became irrelevant, since there was nothing familiar left to which to return.

There was little to be done but accept: I too would wander, like those characters I had envied in my storybooks. There would be new faces, new foods, new vistas at the end of new streets, new words in languages other than those of my childhood, new references to histories that were not mine. I had wished for novelty, change and adventure. Saint Teresa warns us against fulfilled wishes, Blake against nursing unacted desires. Both are right.

In a certain sense, I was already prepared for a

nomadic existence. For the Jews, accustomed to a life of expulsions and re-establishments, the immutable centre is the Bible, which is fixed in time, not in space, and which means (we are told) not "the Book" but "the books," in the plural. Books were for me too a home, a safe place to which I could return no matter where I was taken. In strange bedrooms in Cyprus, Rome or Montevideo, when voices I had not heard before spoke in whispers outside the window and odd scents and curious lights drifted across the newly painted ceilings, my books (from which I would not be parted) would fall open on the familiar pages that told the story of the Seven Swans, of Till Eulenspiegel, of the clever Odysseus, of the Wishing Chair, of Gerda and Kay, of Sindbad and of Mowgli. My eyes followed the words but I knew the texts by heart, even though, from time to time, a new line would appear as if by magic, an unexpected detail would reveal itself in the memorized illustrations, as if (like my body in the mirror) my books grew with me from night to night, faintly but surely, faithful to my end.

A story I enjoyed as a child was that of Puss in the seven-league boots, which allowed the creature to wander the earth regardless of seas or borders. Looking back, my journey (like that of the booted cat) seems surprisingly clear, step after seven-league step.

After Buenos Aires came Spain, because the ship (the cheapest way of transport in those days) stopped in Algeciras; an invitation by a stranger who had (he told me) known Kafka, led me to Paris; from Paris, London seemed like the obvious next stop; austere immigration officials forced me to leave London and return to Paris; a translation of a Borges story into English prompted an invitation from an Italian publisher to come and work for him in Milan; the opening of a bookstore in France took me back once more to Paris; a client buying books for the Tahitian branch of Hachette offered me the chance to leave Europe and settle in the South Seas as a publisher of travel books; the closure of the company, many years later, forced me to decide between setting up in Japan (where a printer had offered me a job), San Francisco (where the Tahitian company was planning to reopen) and Canada (where for aleatory reasons a book of mine had been published). Since I no longer wanted to work in an office but longed instead to try and make my living as a writer, I chose Canada. I was thirty-four years old.

Canada existed nowhere in my imagination before I got here. Canada had drifted, faint and unpretentious, through some of my reading: an Atwood story, an essay by Northrop Frye, a chapter by Saul Bellow, or even more clearly and yet still unobtrusively in the Jalna saga that delighted my aunts or the biography of Graham Bell that sat in my father's library. But unlike England or Polynesia, Japan or France, Canada had failed to conjure up a solid landscape in my dreams. Like one of those places whose existence we assume from a name on a sign above a platform, glimpsed as our train stops and then rushes on, the word "Canada" awoke no echoes, inspired no images, lent no meaning to my port of destination. Canada was the place in which my publisher had her office—nothing more.

I arrived with my family at Pearson Airport on the twenty-second day of October of the year 1982. My son had been born six weeks earlier. As if to rid himself of any small past he might have carried inside him and to begin afresh in this new world, his first act upon landing was to vomit on the carpet outside the immigration bureau.

Our first apartment in Toronto was on George Street, off Queen Street East, opposite a garage that a few months later suddenly burst into flames. It was a tiny place on the second floor of a narrow house, with a cabin kitchen, a small living room, a single bedroom in which the three children slept together, and a minuscule mezzanine that doubled as a second bedroom and my office. Through the children's window they could see the blue *M* of the Bank of Montreal Tower lit up at night so as to lend my eldest daughter the illusion that our family initial was emblazoned against the Toronto sky.

Slowly we began to claim the city's geography: the seedy yet welcoming second-hand stores on Queen Street, the (to us) impressive shoppers' mosque of the Eaton Centre, the tree-lined streets of the Annex (which reminded me of my own street in Buenos Aires), the wonders of Harbourfront and the islands, and Riverdale Park with its inner-city farm full of cows and chickens who would, a couple of years later, become our neighbours, once we had moved to Geneva Avenue, a few steps away from the ravine.

The city in which you grow up grows with you: the height of doors and windows changes as you change, and through the years you continue to know, even if you no longer see them, the cracks and patches of colour that were once at the level of your eyes. There is one system of measures for the room in which you stepped out of your shorts and into your long trousers, where you graduated from games on the floor to games on the desk, where you were promoted from early bed-hours and allowed at long last to stay awake and have dinner with the grown-ups—and a different one for that other room which you enter fully formed, past all true transformation, an adult in a world of adults. (When I managed to buy the house in Cabbagetown, after signing the papers and holding in my hand the document that apparently proved that the place was truly mine, I stood for a long moment in the living room, as if seeing my books and pictures and bits of furniture for the first time, feeling that they were, like myself, strangers in a strange land. Then, somewhat self-consciously, I crouched down to the eye level of a child and looked around me, after which I lay down on the wooden floor and looked up at the empty ceiling, and remembered how many times, when I was four or five, I had done exactly that, in order to see my room upside down with nothing in it, a blank to fill with whatever I wanted, whatever I loved or whatever held my fancy.)

We all took to the city (and to Canada) in different ways. My daughters, who had spent their first years in Tahiti, scuttling barefoot along the beach with packs of other children, would stubbornly kick off their unaccustomed shoes in a snowstorm, and still, from time to time, wear flowers behind their ears. My son, however, when he was old enough, took almost immediately to baseball in the summer and, in the winter, to making snow angels or riding down the ravine slope on a large plastic disc, and later, of course, to hockey. I missed the café life I had known in Argentina and in Europe, the political discussions, the adventurous uncertainty of the economy (which in those days, in Argentina, produced an inflation rate of 200 percent), the late dinners and loud streets. Perhaps I did not really miss these things. Perhaps every newcomer senses the need to feel nostalgic, to lay before himself a photo album of that which he believes he has left behind. The faces may be hazy, the names only vaguely remembered, the voices dim, but he still thinks: "Things are not as good as they were under the reign of Cynara."

Both for myself and for my family, everything was unknown. My siblings in Buenos Aires had the same everyday references as their sons and daughters: they belonged to the same soccer club and read the same comic strips, sang the same nursery rhymes and told the same jokes. I had to learn at the same time as my children about Zambonis and first bases, doughnuts and Slurpees, about the dangers of licking a frozen metal pole and of jaywalking, about Mr. Dressup and Wayne Gretzky, as well as the names of our prime ministers and of the Canadian provinces *a mari usque ad mare.*

My children had little with which to compare the experience, my eldest daughter being only six when we arrived. I, however, felt constantly astounded by the relentless newness of it all. At the end of the Book of Deuteronomy, it is told that God led Moses from the Moabite plains to the mountaintops, and from there showed him the Promised Land that would one day belong to his children but that Moses himself would never possess. There will always be some aspect, some occurrence, some word or event in this country I now call mine that suddenly pulls me back, forces me outside, if only for a moment, to see it once more with the eyes of a foreigner: a view from the land of Moab. This does not happen often, but it happens. For someone who has lived in the chaotic worlds of Argentina, France, Italy, Spain and French Polynesia, with all their ordinary mad behaviour, the civil awareness and tidy obedience of the Canadian citizen appears as a different and far more astounding madness. During my first few years in Canada there were moments that seemed utterly unreal.

Shortly after my arrival in Toronto, I was riding a street-car down Queen Street in a blizzard. At one of the stops a young man got on and showed his transfer ticket. The driver told him it was no longer valid and asked him to pay a new fare. The man refused. The driver insisted. At last the man ripped off a handful of transfers from in front of the driver and stormed off into the snow. The driver got up, told us he'd only be a minute and followed the man down the street. We waited quietly.

Presently, they came back accompanied by a policeman. The driver climbed back into his seat, and the policeman, turning the young man to face us, said to him in a stern but polite tone, "Now you apologize to these good people." And to my amazement, the young man did.

Friends of mine had a small daughter and, because both of them worked full time, decided to employ a Mexican au pair. Canadians are, by and large, terribly ill at ease with "domestic help." They are uncertain of what role to play as employers, how to behave, what to say. My friends decided that, in order not to show any class distinctions, they would treat the young woman as one of the family. They shared their meals with her, invited her to watch television with them in the evenings, asked her to join them when they went out with friends.

One day my mother, who had come over for a visit and had been kindly invited by my friends to lunch, followed the au pair into the kitchen and chatted away to

*her in Spanish. Suddenly the young woman asked if she
could beg a favour.*

"Of course," said my mother.

*"Please, señora, don't think I'm ungrateful. They
are nice, they want me to eat with them, watch TV with
them, go out with them after my work. But señora, I'm
so tired. Could you please tell them to leave me alone?"*

*For a while I tried writing scripts for the CBC. One got
produced, an episode in a series of stories on immigration, and I was asked to write another one. I suggested a
story set among the Haitian taxi drivers in Montreal. My
producer liked the idea but remarked that, since the
theme was Haitian and I clearly was not, it might be best
to work with a writer from that country. I needed the
money, so I accepted, and was lucky enough to be paired
with Dany Laferrière. The plot involved the racist owner
of a taxi company and required that he blurt out a number of racist remarks.*

*When we presented the first draft, the producer was
horrified. "You can't use the word* nigger *on television!"*

*"But the character is a racist," we argued. "That's
what he would say."*

*"Well, you can't use it. Why don't you find some-
thing else, less offensive?"*

"Like what?" we asked.

"Oh, like 'coloured person,'" suggested the producer.

Dany's eyes sparkled. "OK," he said with a danger-ous grin.

And in the episode, the racist boss, furious at his black employee, seems to choke on the words before he splutters, "You . . . you . . . you . . . coloured person!" *The comic effect was stupendous.*

In fact, these astonishing episodes should not have astonished me. Civil manners irrespective of the occasion, utmost consideration for what the Germans laconically call *Gastarbeiter* or "guest workers," offi-cially instituted care not to offend another's sensibili-ties: all these things that should be taken for granted in any society that dares call itself civilized surprised me in Canada because I had not encountered them elsewhere except by chance, in certain individuals, and not as the accepted social code of an entire nation. When many years later my son attended high school in England, he was amazed at the prejudice that manifested itself daily through comments on race, religion, sexuality and class. Not that such things were unknown to him in Canada, but, though the bleak prospect appears on the horizon from time to time (the dark clouds of Ralph Klein, of Mike Harris, of Stockwell Day for instance), at least until now it has never been the official, generalized rule, a fact of everyday life.

Even more astonishing to me was the seemingly endless generosity of this country. Long ago, at the Frankfurt Book Fair, after a chance encounter at the Canadian stand, Margaret Atwood and Graeme Gibson had said to me, "Come to Canada someday." I did not realize how sincere the invitation was until I arrived and enjoyed their help and friendship. Louise Dennys and Ric Young opened the doors of their house to us and let us live there until we found our own place. Geoff Hancock, then editor of *Canadian Fiction Magazine,* unselfishly introduced me to poets and editors. Jack Kapica asked me to write for *The Globe and Mail* merely on the strength of a positive review of my *Dictionary of Imaginary Places.* Damiano Pietropaolo invited me to produce a program for *Ideas,* which began a long relationship with the CBC. Renée Pellerin, with more confidence in my critical abilities than I had myself, gave me my first opportunity on television. Marq de Villiers offered to publish my translation of a Borges story in *Toronto Life.* John Krizanc, in a fit of absent-mindedness, suggested that I write for the theatre, which led

Richard Rose to workshop my *Kipling Play* twice: first with a wonderful cast that included Maggie Huculak, Tanja Jacobs and Stewart Arnott, and then again at the Stratford Festival. Bernadette Sulgit commissioned my first piece for *Saturday Night* where, later, Barbara Moon with uncompromising tenacity tried to teach me how to write journalism that was not pure fiction. Karen Mulhallen called me up and told me she'd like me to write for *Descant*. John Robert Colombo instructed me on the secret history of Canada. (Since I was familiar with none it, Canada's entire history was of course secret to me.) Geraldine Sherman had me review theatre on her CBC arts show. Michael Creal asked me to teach a course on fantastic literature at York University. And all this in the first couple of years! Never before, in any of the other countries in which I had lived, had I received such a constant, unquestioning outpouring of friendly assistance and encouragement to try something new.

Novelty, opportunity, order, generosity define for me this vast country. But perhaps of all its aspects it is the illusion of democracy that attracts me most to Canada. I say "illusion" because we believe in it but are not quite there yet, and perhaps never will be. When our so-called Liberal government pepper-sprays Canadian citizens to defend the interests of a foreign despot, when it builds a wall around the ancient city of Quebec to protect a group of politicians from the anger of the people, when episodes such as the stoning at Oka still take place, when Canada Customs retains the right to ban books, telling us what we can and can't read, then the definition of *democracy* as applied to Canada must be questioned.

And yet, and yet . . . In spite of such infirmities, nowhere else have I had the sense of truly being a citizen, of feeling truly at home. The Greeks believed that a citizen was he who could claim that his ancestors had shed their blood on the city's soil. Canada makes no such demands. It requires nothing but the contribution of one's own experience. Its virtue (or its magic) lies in this, that it both assimilates and hands back the dowry of its newcomers, so that they can both expend and preserve whatever it is they bring to this country. Perhaps this is possible only because Canada has chosen to keep a low political profile (as reflected in the scarcity of Canadian news in the international press), a vision of cold vast spaces (apparent in the publicity of its tourist board), and a modest and open identity (which excluded it from my earlier imagination), so that in some sense Canada illustrates the Second Law of Thermodynamics as applied to nationalities.

Why do I call Canada my home? After seemingly endless trials and adventures, Ulysses reaches Ithaca, the home he left so long ago that he barely remembers it. Is that old woman his wife? Is that young man his son? Is that toothless dog his dog? What proof does he have that this is not another of Circe's spells, the vision of an imagining, a dream that no longer has the vagueness of a dream? How does he know that the place he now calls home is a place he has come back to? Can a traveller not come upon a foreign shore, to a city in which he has never set foot, and feel a pang of recognition, of acquaintance, suddenly able to guess what lies beyond that distant building and around that farthest corner? Can he not experience the joy of homecoming even if he is returning to a place in which he has never before set foot?

Now, when I think of homeland, I think of Canada. Nowhere else have I been persuaded of sharing in the *res publica*, the "public thing" that has to do with customs and language and landscape, with assumptions and open questions and something like faith in the prevalence of our better qualities. Nowhere else have I wanted to pledge allegiance to a nation, to something beyond the individual, beyond a particular face or name. Nowhere else have I felt the need or the desire to claim myself part of a society whose brand new Constitution still declares its belief in what (in another of my constant childhood books) Robert Louis Stevenson once called "an ultimate decency of things."

Michelle Berry

—

BETWEEN TWO THANKSGIVINGS

SIX YEARS OLD AND running free in the fields in Virginia.

Seven years old and sitting two weeks in a moving van as we drive across the United States.

Seven years old and standing on the ferry to Victoria, my hair blowing into my eyes, watching the vast ocean, the many islands, my brother standing beside me, the solid presence of Canada all around.

I step on the boat an American. I walk off the boat a Canadian landed immigrant.

It's funny how I want my memory to work a certain way. I want it to be like those history classes I took in high school, chronological and ordered, completely straightforward. Dates combined with facts create a moment in time. But memory doesn't work that way. It's not a connected line; instead it's a series of images flashing on my consciousness, images that are connected only by a thread of thought. It's a chain reaction. Tip over one domino and the rest will fall down.

In the middle of June 1975 my family packed up a U-Haul moving van, the biggest on the lot. We also packed up our little car. We put everything we had into these two vehicles (cat, toys, dishes, furniture, bedding, clothes) and left our small house in Stony Point, Virginia, for a two-week adventure through the United States. We were the Beverly Hillbillies. We were cowboys. We were pioneers in our stagecoaches and we were the settlers. My brother was nine. I was seven. I had just played the role of Betsy Ross in my grade one end-of-year school play. I remember some complicated manoeuvre the teacher taught me where, as I pretended to sew a blank piece of white cloth, I would turn my hand slightly and push the American flag up through the cloth. From plain white to red, white and blue. It was my first and last magic trick.

Americans have been coming to Canada for a good long time and for all sorts of reasons. During the Civil War in the 1860s, Americans dodged the draft and many settled in New Brunswick in a place referred to as Skedaddle Ridge. (During World War I it was the opposite, America providing a safe refuge for those Canadians who didn't want to enlist to fight overseas.) In the late 1950s, U.S. academics started moving to

Canada when Canada was expanding its universities and founding new ones. About 125,000 Americans came to Canada between 1964 and 1977 as draft dodgers of the Vietnam War. Half of them stayed.

Back and forth. The borders touch. It's one big mass of land. There's no getting around it.

My father had taken a job at the University of Victoria as an English professor. On our glass coffee table, before we left, he laid out a map of the United States and Canada and my brother and I kneeled down to trace the route we would take: through Pennsylvania, through the Midwest to Chicago, through Iowa and the Badlands and Wyoming or Montana (nobody's sure any more), through Idaho to Washington state, where we would take the Anacortes ferry to Victoria and touch down (all of us—our toys, the U-Haul, the poor carsick cat) on Canadian soil. My father told us about Victoria. He told us about living on an island. He told us about the Queen and my seven-year-old mind pictured a Disney-style monarch with a Cinderella past—both suffering and noble. He showed us how big Canada was. When he told us about the vastness of Canada, we saw the huge expanse of colours on the map, hardly any of it covered in writing. Somehow I understood that the journey would be a big one, and that the line my father traced across the country was not really an arm-span long but stretched for miles and miles and miles.

At that time I imagined we were going some-where temptingly exotic, somewhere outside of any experience I had ever had. Having read *Pippi Longstocking,* I wondered if Canadians would walk backwards or, even better, walk on their hands. I was looking for adventure. The fact that the neighbouring kids didn't know where Canada was made it even more exciting. "We're moving to Canada," I would say to the little girl down the street as she stood in her driveway surrounded by chickens. We were leaving grandparents and aunts and uncles and cousins in New Jersey (where, at Thanksgiving dinners, we would all congregate, the men, unbuckled, watching football on TV, the women chattering away in the kitchen, the kids running haywire around my grand-parents' home). We were leaving people we loved, my career as Betsy Ross, my ballet class, the fields and woods around our house.

The Vietnam War was over, Watergate was winding down. My parents had friends who had trained their one-year-old to stick out his tongue and blow noisily at Nixon whenever he was on TV.

My parents had done this kind of mass moving before. My father's Ph.D. is from Berkeley, California (my mother gave birth to my brother and me in a teaching hospital in San Francisco). He then received a Fulbright Scholarship and they shipped off (with two small children) to the U.K. to study in London. Before they had children, my parents taught in Sierra Leone for the Peace Corps. So this kind of relocating was old news for them. They'd packed up their houses and apartments many times to live in other countries, other places. They knew to come prepared: bags of games and toys for each day that we could open in the moving van or car; pop and chips in front of the TV in the motel at night. Start driving at 8 A.M., end at 4 P.M. and, most importantly, always find a motel with a pool. My brother and I were usually separated between the car and the van, each getting to spend time with one parent, each keeping one parent awake (this kept us from bickering with each other). My father taped all our records, and whoever was in the van got to listen to "Jelly on Your Belly" and *The Lone Ranger* over and over.

The van was expansive. My feet didn't touch the floor. My father was omnipotent. There he was controlling this huge beast. I stuck my hand out the window and shot things—a tree, a bird, the land-scape of cars below us. I waved my hand in the wind, an early version of breakdancing. I sang "Leaving on a Jet Plane," because my teenage cousin had taught me it earlier that year as she strummed her guitar.

I remember the Badlands, or at least the photograph of me standing there. I can see the beige short set I was wearing, the scabs on my knees, the dust blowing. I remember the prairie dogs poking out of their holes, arms poised, begging.

The scenery changed. Things became lush (although anything is lush after the dust bowls of the Prairies). The motels were nicer, the pools clean. There was something coming, bright, just around the corner. Anticipation was thick in the air. We were approaching Canada.

We weren't running from persecution, we weren't leaving because we had to, we weren't com-ing to Canada for good. We would return to the States, we reasoned, in a couple of years. We spoke the same language as Canadians. We had come from a democracy to a democracy. My father had a guar-anteed job. He was an academic. I was blonde and blue-eyed. I'd memorized all the states and their cap-itals. I knew the U.S. presidents. We'd fit right in.

The ferry docked July 1, 1975. If you know Vancouver Island, you'll know that it was probably raining. My mother had clam chowder at a local pub in Sidney while the customs officers went over our moving van. She remembers that, what she ate. I don't know what I ate or what I felt like or what I was thinking. I was tired. Two weeks on the road, no matter how many bags of toys you get or swimming pools you dive into, or sodas to drink, potato chips to eat, takes its toll on a seven-year-old. There was a need for home, for stability, for somewhere to put down those bags of toys.

The first house we rented had a balcony attached to my second-floor room. I would stand on the balcony and look down at my brother as he and his new friends would ride in circles on their bikes, trying to make me dizzy. My father played the trumpet and the jazz sounds would echo around the walls.

The summer we arrived, my brother and I on our bikes with a gang of kids from the neighbourhood, we weren't different. Once I got here, everything around me said that things wouldn't be different in Canada. I had new bell-bottom jeans like the kid down the street. I had long hair I wore in pigtails just like every other girl I saw. I went from riding bikes with banana seats and streamers in Virginia to riding bikes with banana seats and streamers in Victoria. Both places started with a V. All was the same.

Then came Mrs. Harrington's grade two class. Oaklands Elementary School. We were a pretty bright class. At least we liked being there in grade two: no one had dropped out yet and the kids weren't smoking behind the school during recess. (Not in grade two. Grade four, maybe.) We had a nurturing older teacher. I listened to the class sing "O Canada" and say the Lord's Prayer every morning. I kept waiting for the national anthem. When did we "pledge allegiance to the flag of the United States of America," the flag I had so trickily sewn in that school play—red, white, blue? I would look around, waiting. What was going on?

And then it dawned on me about a month into school that everyone around me knew things I didn't know. The provinces. They knew what provinces were. They even knew the capital cities of the provinces and the lakes and the other big bodies of water. Sure, I was superior—there were many more states than their flimsy little province-count, and I knew them all—but I was suddenly not the same as everyone else and suddenly very far behind. And kids notice that kind of thing. They notice when you pronounce words differently. I remember sitting with a little girl in the school library on one of the first days and everyone laughing at me because I said "orange" differently; I said "R-ange." I also said "toilit paper" and "maalk." The little girl was so nervous that day that she threw up all over the library books spread out in front of us. I remember the smell. But no one noticed, because I was the novelty of the day.

Years ago my mother was accused of having an Australian accent. Her New Jersey drawn-out a's and r's mellow with the length of time she spends in Victoria. When she goes home to visit her family, she comes back sounding like she never left the States. It takes a week or two to fade. I notice my slight accent (just on certain words) when I'm giving readings. The American twang to my speech seems to fit my writing, seems destined to be part of how I think.

"Yankee," the kids said on the second day. They must have gone home and told their parents about me. Tensions between Canada and the U.S. were relatively high at that point. Academics like my father were being written up in the newspapers as having taken jobs away from Canadians. The year before we came to Canada, there was an amendment to the immigration act which stated that if there was a qualified Canadian applicant to a post-secondary institution, he or she should be considered before a foreign applicant. Even with this amendment, there was still a strong fear that the universities would become Americanized. There was also ripe, fetid anger against Americans following the horrible truths about the Vietnam War. After all, the draft dodgers (mostly middle-class, educated, white young men, who assimilated quickly into Canadian culture) had fled here and were working and living in Canada. The facts of Vietnam were coming out.

So we were the "Yanks."

This, of course, is the history I remember. This is something that has no corresponding photograph I can refer to.

I remember rapidly learning the provinces, trying desperately to catch up to the rest of the class. By Christmas I was cast as Mary in the nativity play we were doing at school. There is a photograph of me, kneeling down in front of the cradle, my head swathed in a veil (a soft white towel, it looks like), wearing a blue dress. There are kids to the left of me, to the right of me, Joseph and the three wise men standing there looking lost, a choir singing. How did I earn the right to be in the centre of all of this? Between September and December had I started to pronounce words correctly? Had I stopped being a Yankee? Did the teachers feel sorry for me? Or maybe it was just one of those times where the new kid has to do the thing that no one else wants to do.

I had friends. I had best friends. I rushed to school early every morning to play floor hockey. I hung around with the crowd who chased the boys, and I played a big part in getting them to kiss us. I joined a baseball team and did cartwheels out in centre field. In the beginning of grade three I remember Mrs. Harrington died. And that broke my heart. This elderly British woman had taken me in and made me feel as if I had arrived somewhere, as if I were finally home. She never once corrected my accent or made me feel different.

By the end of grade three I was quickly forgetting the States. I forgot everything I had ever learned. My grandparents visited from New Jersey every year, and one year they brought me a Betsy Ross pincushion doll.

"Who's Betsy Ross?" I asked my mother as I flipped up the skirt to see what you poked pins into.

We never moved away from Victoria, but we travelled quite a few summers to the States—California and Washington, D.C.—for my father's research for the books he was writing. We went to New Jersey for Christmas one year and were spoiled rotten by my grandparents because we were suddenly distinct, different from our cousins. Or maybe it was just because we lived so far away and they missed us. We were spoiled with Haddenfield cream doughnuts, a delicacy that, in memory, still causes my mouth to water and makes me remember my grandparents. (A little aside: When visiting my grandparents on my own when I was in university, I froze a Haddenfield cream doughnut and mailed it to my brother, who was living in Vancouver. Just one little doughnut. He said it arrived all mushy, probably stale, but he ate it anyway. He knew the importance of the gesture. He knew that something small like that still carried so much weight.)

My parents became Canadian citizens in 1988 and 1989, and my brother and I followed some years later. My brother was actually registered for the draft in the U.S. from age eighteen to twenty-six. The Selective Service System had tracked him down, just in case. They thanked him when he turned twenty-six and let him go with a letter that said his "registration was an important part of America's peacetime military preparedness [and] played a part in maintaining peace and protecting the citizens of our Nation and their freedom."

I asked my father recently if he felt he was Canadian and he immediately answered yes. I wonder about this myself. What would I say if my daughters asked me if I felt Canadian?

As a writer in Canada, or anywhere else probably, your work gets labelled—mystery writer, science fiction writer, literary writer, gay writer, etc. And then there are the books that branch out and try on new labels—literary thriller, science fiction romance, etc. Living in Toronto now, I'm automatically a "Toronto writer." I've even received reviews condemning me for where I live. Once you start selling to the United States and other countries, you are also a "Canadian writer," even if you're originally from India or Africa or Australia and are writing about that country. If you've immigrated to Canada, if you hold citizenship or landed immigrant status and live here, you are Canadian. I am a Canadian writer.

This is a strange way of belonging to a country. As an immigrant to this country I am alive to the differences that surround me, the differences that are a part of me. I don't know anything about hockey, really, I can't get my head around it. Nor do I understand curling. I played baseball as a kid and was pretty good at it.

There are ironies in the Canadian personality

which I find fascinating and my neighbours seem not even to notice. Cultured and polite Canadians, sophisticated Canadians, turn into maniacs during the Stanley Cup playoffs. Canadians who claim not to be patriotic will preach the merits of Canadian beer, heaping derision on the American product. But then, on Oscar night, Canadians will gather around television sets, desperate to know who has won this American gold statue. And in the arts it is a well-known fact that you haven't really "made it" until you make it in the States. In fact, the Canadian personalities who go South end up being literally sucked, like a dip in quick-sand, into their new country. And then what happens? Years later, when we are reminded that this Super-Famous-So-and-So is Canadian it amazes us. "Really? No way!" Don't think I haven't noticed.

These perspectives can be seen as American. But am I really American either? When I go to the United States now, what I notice are the little things—the little things those kids at Oaklands Elementary School noticed in me. The food portions are always bigger in the States. Everything is bigger actually, television ads seem bigger and brighter. If I were really an American, these things wouldn't seem bigger; they would seem just right.

The point here is that I am a combination of both nationalities. But, even more importantly, I am also neither. I occupy a space outside both countries that lends me a perspective that I think has facilitated my career as a writer. I can be a stranger in my own country. I can watch both Canada and the United States with fascination and curiosity. I can step back and watch. Not quite fitting in gives me the advantage of being able to undertake a kind of scientific examination of culture and people in an artistic way. I have the lucky position of an observer; I don't really have to work on it. And as a writer is naturally an observer, the path I've chosen to walk down is nicely maintained. Paved, even.

It's a constant blending. Memory and identity. It's interesting that my mother, my father, my brother and I all decided to remain dual citizens. My brother teaches now in Barbados and he tells his students that he's 100 percent Canadian. And 100 percent American. But if he is totally both, then, if you really think about it, he is neither.

My brother reminds me of the one year we celebrated two Thanksgivings. He says we ate turkey leftovers, stuffing, turkey sandwiches, cranberry sauce, for months. I think we had something else for Christmas dinner, maybe a ham. And I remember the time I was shopping with my mom in the grocery store in October and she looked up and noticed the Thanksgiving decorations hanging from the ceiling and rushed to buy a turkey. The two dates—October or November?—played havoc with our holidays for years. My brother also remembers being mixed up about the songs at school "My country 'tis of thee . . . God save the Queen."

It all has to do, really, with when I came to Canada. I came when I was seven years old. One of my daughters is five now, and I ask myself, if in two years we moved away from Canada, would she know anything about Canadian politics or history, about the cultural mosaic or Canadian immigration policies? No. She would know what I knew: the small differences, the minute things that made me stand apart and still make me feel individual. Home for me is exactly the spot where my family is right now.

I think this Canadian/American thing, this blending, has made my family closer than we might have been had we stayed put in Virginia. My mother and father left their own families to move to Canada, and so our tight-knit family became everything we knew. Holiday dinners were only the four of us. We were different from those other families in Canada with their big get-togethers, and we slowly became different from those other families in the United States, different from the relatives we had left behind. So we had to stay together. We are some strange new breed—neither a part of where we came from nor a part of where we are now.

I've been playing dominoes here with my memory. I've knocked one over, and a whole row has gathered speed and fallen over all around me.

There's a photo of me on the ferry, arms open wide. I'm wearing flowered pants, a long jacket. My brother is smiling. His face is happy and content. But where's my face? My hair is in my face. Long hair blowing around my head, covering my eyes, my mouth. You have to look twice to see which direction I'm facing. You have to notice the little knee bumps and the way my hands turn. You have to look closely to see the bit of forehead peeking out of the wind-whipped hair. I'm sailing forward but looking back. Caught in a moment between two countries. Not knowing the differences that lie ahead but obviously enjoying that in-between stage that I seem to have stayed in my entire life.

———

Shyam Selvadurai

——

CONVERSATIONS WITH MY MOTHER

IN 1975, MY PARENTS made a significant trip to America. My father was taking my mother so that she could decide if she would like to live there. He was a tennis coach and, for the past few years, had been teaching at a prestigious Massachusetts country club. They were now offering him full-time work. My mother was a doctor. By sitting for a simple exam (simple for her, anyway, as she had a real knack for exams) she could re-qualify as a doctor. The lifestyle they were contemplating was definitely an upper-middle-class one, with very few of the stresses and strains most immigrants face upon arrival in a new country. The decision was entirely up to my mother. Whatever she wanted, my father would abide by it.

She said no.

I telephone my mother to ask her why she said no all those years ago. Her answer is only one word:

"lifestyle." Her voice lingers over the *l*, drawing it out in a quiet sigh. Immediately an image rises in my mind.

We are at the swimming club, clouds like gauze scarves fluttering in the blue sky. My mother slowly descends the steps into the water. "Ma-Ma-Mummy!" We children make a furious dash across the pool towards her, each determined to get there first. She raises her hand, palm outwards. A nervous swimmer, she does not like being splashed. I am the best non-splasher. As my mother glides out and down the pool, her head above the water, I stay as close to her as I can. I love the feel of her legs kicking the water behind us, the smell of her perfume mingled with the chlorine on her skin. To me there is no one more beautiful than my mother in her purple one-piece bathing suit.

Later, when the sun is too fierce for swimming, we will return home. Sunday lunch is always special. Even while paddling in the water, I can almost taste the explosion of flavours in my mouth—the buttery yellow rice scattered with sultanas and cashews, nutty eggplant moju, succulent chicken curry, devil shrimp, dal, fish cutlets, and chocolate biscuit pudding for dessert. We come running into the house ahead of my mother, go to wash our hands, take our places at the table. We bow our head for grace. My father thanks

God for our meal, for the fact that we have food. It never crosses his mind, or indeed strikes any of us, to offer up thanks to the maid who laid the table, to the cook who made this lunch.

My mother, on the other end of the telephone, breaks into my reverie. "Then there was the Lodge."

The Lodge. Or to give it its full name, the Ibis Safari Lodge.

My father was a man who took his great loves and turned them into money. Even before I was born, he abandoned the steady climb up the corporate ladder that his schooling and family background ensured. He had played Davis Cup for Sri Lanka and had been the national tennis champion, and he decided to go to Australia and qualify as a tennis coach. His other great passion was wildlife, and in the early seventies he became the first person in Sri Lanka to offer safaris. So successful was this venture that he built a hotel—the Lodge—to house his tourists.

How I used to love going to the Lodge, beginning with the journey in the open Jeep. Our route took us first through the lush foliage and rivers of the wet zone of Sri Lanka, then the road emerged onto the coastline and we would travel past miles and miles of white beach, turquoise water. The change of scenery, as it always is in Sri Lanka, was dramatic. We always stopped at Tangalle Bay for a picnic lunch, which we children would eat quietly, hoarse by now from screaming out jokes and mild obscenities at the village children we had passed.

Within an hour from Tangalle the landscape completely changed again. We entered the dry zone. The hazy, moisture-laden yellow light of the wet zone gave way to brilliant clear whiteness (the same quality of light as a dazzling February day in Toronto). The trees on the sides of the road were stunted, with few leaves, yet filled with brilliant red and orange flowers. Vast arid plains stretched into the distance, a smell of dried clay pervading the air.

To get to the Lodge, our Jeep would then leave the main road and go along a narrow jungle path. So close were the trees that we had to sit on the floor of the Jeep to escape the thorny branches which banged and rattled against the sides. When we were in the clear, we rose quickly to our feet, and there it was. The Lodge. A long wooden building, it boasted an extensive deck with pillars at regular intervals supporting the low-slung roof. Doors led off the deck into the bedrooms. The building was raised eight feet off the ground, for in the rainy season the Wirawilla lake lapped at the base of the Lodge, with flamingos, painted storks, peacocks, buffalo, and deer, even an occasional elephant, along its distant banks. In the dry season all this animal life receded to the centre, around a water hole.

What adventures we children had at the Lodge. If the tank was full, there was fishing and bathing. The tank had man-eating crocodiles in it, though, so we always stayed in the shallows, one of us keeping an eye out for the deceptive logs. In the dry season we would play cricket or badminton on the parched floor of the tank, and make treks to the water hole to see the wildlife. We would go into the jungle, my brother leading the way with his air rifle, and thrill with terror when we came upon fresh elephant dung.

While the Lodge is, in my mind, associated with all that was best about my childhood and adolescence, it is also linked indelibly with the beginning of the end.

The Lodge was in the deep south of Sri Lanka, and my father was from the minority Tamil community. For a Tamil, the Sri Lankan south has the same implications as the American south for an African-American. Friends of my father had advised against his building the Lodge. Yet my father loved the south. This was his country, and he would go wherever he wanted in it.

In 1977, for the first time in my life, ethnic conflict broke out between the Sinhalese and Tamils. For people who, like us, lived in the capital, Colombo, this conflict could seem removed, as it was confined mainly to the south and other regions of the country. And so it might have seemed for us too, if it weren't for the Lodge: my brother was there, on vacation. For a few days we did not know if he was alive or dead. All I remember of that time was the way the world seemed to slow down. My mother told us to keep busy, to pray. But I remember lying on my bed, conscious of the hours dragging on. Finally the telephone call came to say that he was safe. The mob had indeed come to the Lodge demanding him, but the staff had spirited him away into the jungle. If the mob had found him, they would have butchered him with the sharp scythes they brought with them or, worse, put a tire around his neck, poured kerosene over him and set him on fire. He was only fourteen years old.

The mob burnt the Lodge, right down to its foundation. Somebody else might have backed off, given up, but when my father saw the charred, broken remains of the this thing he had loved, a determination was sealed in him. My mother pleaded against it, but he went back and rebuilt the Lodge. In an act of solidarity a Sinhalese friend, a building contractor, provided all the materials and labour for free. Yet in the end the new Lodge was a diminished version of what had been. For one thing, my father felt compelled to build it out of bricks and cement, for obvious reasons. In the years that followed, the signboard directing travellers to the Lodge was frequently pulled down, vandalized, defecated on. After the scare with my brother, my parents rarely took us with them, and when we did go, we stayed close to the Lodge. In our treks into the jungle we had always been aware of the dangers—the poisonous snakes, the wild buffalo, the wild boar—but they had not kept us from exploring. However, none of these was as terrifying as the savagery of men.

In 1981, rioting broke out again, and the Lodge was destroyed. My father learned the news on the afternoon of his birthday. It was too late to cancel the party. That evening, as our garden filled with guests, resembled a funeral. Among the guests was a Canadian, a Jewish emigrant from Nazi Germany. He told my father that what was happening in Sri Lanka reminded him of those dreadful times, and he advised my father to leave. My father vacillated, said he would think about it later. I remember being furious with him for not taking us away, feeling frightened and sad at how our lives were falling apart. Now that I am in my thirties, I understand why my father could not go. He loved the country, had invested himself in it and made a life for himself there.

The fear, the terror of this ethnic conflict was like a beast circling ever closer. It finally did strike us, in 1983, when the rioting spilled over into Colombo. Mobs of Sinhalese went on a rampage, destroying Tamil houses, dragging families out of hiding and butchering them. They were in possession of electoral lists which they used to single out the Tamil homes. They also destroyed Tamil-owned shops and offices. Our personal experience of it is too painful to narrate here. We lost everything. My parents applied to Canada under a program of accelerated immigration that was being offered to Tamils wishing to leave. Our papers came through and we left for Canada in 1984.

Nine years after my parents had decided to forego an affluent lifestyle in the West in order to live out their passions and their commitment to the country of their birth, they found themselves forced to leave, to come here and start over with nothing.

I am on the telephone to my mother again. I want to know if she has any regrets about not going to America all those years ago. She is silent for a while.

In the background I can hear the grandchildren, some loud game in progress. She is about to speak when one of them interrupts to ask her something. As she talks to him, I can imagine her hand resting against the side of his head. By the time she comes back to the telephone, I already know here answer. Yet she surprises me as she elaborates on it.

"America is too dynamic. Everything there is hire-and-fire. Here things are more low-key, one is allowed to develop at one's own pace. Canada is a more accommodating society." Again she is silent. "But darling, it was hard." How laden her voice is as she draws out the "hard."

My mind slips back to our first year here.

It is that day in October when you know that the world around you has turned irreversibly towards winter. All last night the wind clattered against our windows, torn at the sides of the house, the rain a battering of angry fists. Now a weak sun sheds its light on shorn trees, their naked branches like arms stretched upwards in hunger, the newly fallen leaves blackened clots on the grass.

My mother returns home, trembling with humiliation. At an office where she has temporary work, there was a party at lunchtime. She had brought something, expecting to share in the potluck meal. Yet just before the lunch hour her supervisor came to her. "You can go on break now. We're having a party."

As my mother sits at the dining table telling us this story, a helpless rage takes hold of me, a rage I see reflected in the face of my father and siblings. Even before we arrived in this country, my mother had already accepted that she would never be able to practise medicine here. Unlike in America, where she would have had only to sit an exam, here she would have to do an internship as well, and there are a mere handful of internships for all the foreign doctors applying. The bar is set unfairly high. My mother has also realized that to say she is a doctor on her resumé intimidates people who might hire her. She has "doctored" it down, first to a Bachelor of Science and finally to housewife.

I look at my mother this day as if seeing her after a long absence. She is of that first generation of modern Sri Lankan women, imbued with a sense of confidence that her gender will not hold her back, living out the fruits of the struggles of the women before her. As a Sri Lankan woman, she could stand tall. But here in Canada she is learning to be small, subservient, docile, to fit the society's expectations of an Asian woman. In the few months we have been here, she has not so much aged physically as withered inside, developed a stoop of her shoulders.

As if my mother has sensed my thoughts over the phone, she says, "But this country *has* been good to us, you children in particular. All of you have done well. As for the medicine"—she *has* read my thoughts—"I might not have pursued it anyway. Your sister was only thirteen when we came here. If I was preoccupied with my career, who knows what trouble she might have got up to."

Yet my parents now go back to Sri Lanka for half the year, have bought a house there. They have returned to their first love. I wonder if my mother's answers would be different if they had been unable to re-establish a partial life there, if they lived only with the raw nerve-endings-cut-off longing for it.

After I put down the phone, I drift towards the kitchen, out through the patio doors and into the garden. My cat follows as we both go, trail-trail, through the grass. What I am trying so hard to remember are my first impressions of Canada. The truth of the matter is that when I think of myself as I was then, it is like looking at a person with one's glasses off; there is a blurring of outlines, a smudge of features. It will be some time before I come back into my focus in my memory.

I bend down to move aside a broken branch, the cat seizing the opportunity to run up rub herself against my hand, when suddenly, with a small "oh," something rises in my mind.

It is our second week in Canada. We are staying with my uncle in Richmond Hill. So far I have not ventured further than the nearby Hillcrest Mall. This will be my first trip downtown. My uncle is carefully going over the instructions he has written down. I struggle to pay attention. My hands in my pockets are slick with sweat; I can feel a coldness down the back of my neck. I am terrified that my uncle, my family, will ask where I am going, terrified that my voice will crack as I deliver the carefully practised lie. But everyone is too preoccupied with their own adjustments to this new country.

When I finally leave my uncle's house, I feel as if I am escaping a stifling room. I breathe deeply as I walk up the road to the bus stop. Part of me wants to turn back, to be released from this commitment, but a far sterner part keeps me going. I have waited too long to turn back.

My adolescence in Sri Lanka was darkened by a shadow—a failure, I thought, within myself. While other boys would sit around bragging about their conquests with girls and fantasizing, I sat with them in silence, trying not to stare at the curve of their necks, the way their thighs flexed and strained against the thin cotton of their pants. The word "ponnaya" was dispensed with an upward curl of the lips, a fiery contempt in one's eyes. I slowly came to realize that this word applied to a person like myself.

Over the years of hiding these feelings, I gleaned enough knowledge to be aware that in the West things were a little better for someone like me. Coming to Canada held the promise of a great meeting with the one to whom I could say who I was. I don't know why I thought of it as one person rather than a group.

Now, for the first time, I am on a journey to look for him.

My destination is the Royal Alexandra Theatre. A play called *Torch Song Trilogy* is running there. The waves this play is making in North America had reached me in Sri Lanka through *Time* magazine. It is an explicitly gay-themed work, where homosexuality

is presented without apology, without obfuscation.
I am sure I will find others like myself there, that
somehow a connection will be made.

Standing in the garden, I remember myself with sudden clarity, coming out of St. Andrew subway station, pausing in front of the glass-fronted Sun Life
building, looking at myself for the first time through
somebody else's desire. I am wearing a pair of beige
pants pleated in front, a brown belt and a red jersey
shirt, tucked inside. Yes, there I stand, so terrified at
what the future holds for me, yet my body, my very
being, is transformed by the possibility of someone
else's love. I see myself as I walk along King Street,
across University Avenue, past the Roy Thomson
Hall, towards my destiny.

Alas for my poor post-adolescent self, newly
arrived in this country, I was going to attend a
Wednesday matinee. The only people there were
seniors, busloads of them brought in from I don't
know where for an afternoon on the town. I sat
through the play in a haze of disappointment as the
audience around me tittered and twittered and
belched and fell asleep and ate candy. On the way
back to Richmond Hill, I got lost, took the subway in

the wrong direction, to the end of the line at Wilson station. Then I had to take it all the way back around the loop. I sat there looking at the image of myself flashing by in the window, lit from the fluorescent tube above, my features flattened out, my skin a washed out grey.

I feel a great tenderness for this younger self. He is so painfully thin, the way his neck rises out of his shirt like a lily stalk, his hair so out of style, his very best clothes so shabby in comparison with those of the people around him. Yet at the same time I want to place my hand firmly on his arm. I want to say that this thing he seeks will be an entry not just into himself but also into this country. I want to tell him that the friends he will make through coming out will be the ones who will last; they will be the ones from whom he will learn the norms, the standards, the culture and the history of this country. With them he will attend protest marches, organize to demand the same rights as other Canadians, start to have an investment in this new land. They will be the first people he will tell about Sri Lanka, and thereby he will begin the long process of healing those wounds.

A slight breeze has picked up in the garden now, the leaves of the elm tree shift and sigh, the cat chases after a butterfly, something my mother said returns to me. Before I put down the telephone, her last words were, "Never forget that Canada gave us the enormous privilege of being able to sleep through the night." As I look around at the life I have built in this country, I touch my forehead briefly in salutation.

May that always be so.

———

Anna **Porter**

A CANADIAN EDUCATION

THERE ARE SO MANY other lives I might have lived. Sometimes I feel that I have merely borrowed this one. One day I may have to return it.

There is the life I left behind in Hungary. It's not a terrible life, though there are aspects of it I am glad I have avoided. My aunt Edie, for example, spent ten years in jail because she was judged guilty of taking part in the '56 Revolution. Edie had helped the British embassy staff escape to London after their ill-advised assistance to students. She may also have taken part in the attack on the national radio station.

She's had a hard life, my aunt. Her sons were raised in state-run institutions while she tried to appeal her fate. Her younger son, who is my age, spends most of his time training peregrine falcons. I think he must have watched the birds from his grated window at the orphanage. He is still unsure whether to forgive his mother for missing his childhood.

My mother believed I would have been in that jail too, had we stayed in Budapest after the revolution was lost. A childhood acquaintance was kept there until he was eighteen. Then he was executed.

During my childhood I imagined I was a great Hungarian patriot. The stories I knew were all Hungarian stories. The thought that I would one day live somewhere else, speak another language, would never have occurred to me. I was, most of the time, in the company of my grandfather, a fantastic man who told riveting tales about our history, loved magic, played cheater chess, fought duels with brass-hilted swords, had hundreds of friends all over Budapest, and knew every street corner, every bridge, the remnants of every castle wherever we roamed. My world was circumscribed by the stories he shared with me.

My grandfather had been a book and magazine publisher before the war, but above all, he loved poetry. Poets, he believed, could see the world more clearly than other people. He would recite long narrative poems while he shaved and I waited for our walk to one of his favourite coffee houses, where clandestine writers, revolutionary poets, former journalists, and other enemies of the Communist regime gathered and talked.

Because he was my hero, I wrote poems. Many of them were long, with galloping rhythms and very predictable rhymes. When I finished a poem, I would present it to my grandfather and he would read it, nodding in appreciation. Sometimes he read out loud, slipping around the rhymes, letting the rhythm take care of itself. I think, had we stayed in Hungary, I would have tried to be a poet—perhaps not a particularly good one, but I would have persevered. Hungarians are famous for persevering. That's how their language has survived in a sea of Germans and Slavs.

Since the Iron Curtain was parted, I have returned for visits. In some ways I have tried to reclaim a past and a history I had once imagined filled the world.

I travelled to my grandfather's birthplace in Bácska, now part of Yugoslavia, or Serbia, close to Hungary's southern border. I placed flowers on his parents' graves and sat in the white church where he had first encountered the Transylvanian dragon. I climbed the steep hill to Hunyadvar, the ancient seat of the Hunyadi princes, where my ancestors fought to defend their lord. We had been warrior folk, given to sword fights, fast horses and white-faced women with long brownish tresses. We had always treated dragons with respect.

I went to Tövis, now in Romania, where we thrived for some four hundred years, and tried to find traces of our once fertile lands.

In Budapest, I wandered along the Danube, following my grandfather's footsteps, skirting the Castle, across the bridges from Buda to Pest and back again. I sat in Vörösmarty Square and ate ice cream and chestnut purée in the Gerbaud café. I saluted the Anonymous statue on Margaret Island and studied the blood-coloured portraits of heroic ancestors in the National Gallery. I danced in the middle of Heroes' Square and flirted with the grim faces of the Millennium Monument's seven tribal leaders.

I climbed to the third floor of our old rat-infested apartment building on Rákoczi Street and almost met myself leaping down the wide-angled stairs. I followed myself down to the basement, where there are still woodpiles and coal mounds, but the man whose fingernails had been yanked out doesn't speak to me any more. When I see him in my dreams, his hands are covered by darkness. He no longer frightens me.

In Toronto there are no political prisoners whose nails are extracted, and very few people are beaten to death by the police. When someone dies in custody, there are investigations, newspaper reports, tribunals, and sometimes policemen are sent to jail. In Hungary, when someone went to jail, it was best not to mention that person again. It was safest to pretend he or she had never existed. We lived in a Communist dictatorship. When my mother was in jail, we said she was working on the prairies. When my grandfather was jailed, no one asked about him.

After he had served his time at hard labour, the government allowed him to leave his beloved Hungary. He had agreed to go because he knew he could not remain silent about the regime of terror that ruled the country, and the price one paid for speaking up was to be jailed. He died in exile in New Zealand.

I grew up in New Zealand.

It's one of the world's most beautiful countries, with mountains and pastures, endless ocean vistas, noisy, colourful birds, hot springs and icefields. I think of it as verdant and terrifying in a way Hungary wasn't. In New Zealand, I was scared of being alone. I was alone most of the time. I didn't adapt well to the change. Nor did I ever feel welcome or wanted. New

Zealand, though it may be the most beautiful place in the world, is not hospitable for exiles.

When I go back now, I meet myself swinging down the street in Christchurch, and think about the person I might be, had I stayed and kept trying to fit in. I would most certainly own a good bicycle. I used to ride an old, paint-peeling, bent-handlebarred bike from Ainsley Terrace on the river Avon. I had to stand on the pedals to brake. Once, I was arrested for borrowing another bike—well, I suppose it did seem like theft—and I was charged and fingerprinted. The police sergeant thought I would be frightened by the procedure. "Have you ever been inside a jail before?" he asked me portentously. "Have you ever been in an interrogation room?" I shook my head. No sense in telling him the truth.

Early mornings, I used to pedal to the Princess Margaret Hospital to clean toilets and walls. I would be up at four and out the door in half an hour, dreading the long bike ride along the Avon. I remember keeping to the middle of the half-lit street, away from the shadows cast by the weaving willows. I hated my light green uniform because a Hungarian soothsayer gypsy woman had warned me once to stay away from green. She had insisted that green was my unlucky colour.

I had become rather fond of one of the old ladies on the "mental ward." Most days she would take my face between her dry-fingered hands and tell me what she could see. "There is a scar that starts just here, under your hairline, and it runs across your nose and down to your mouth, catches the corner. It's hard for you to smile, isn't it, dear? Such an angry red scar."

"It doesn't hurt," I would tell her, but she knew better. She smiled her sad, lopsided smile. She had a scar too, and she didn't think there was time for it to heal. She was too old; her skin had lost its resilience. "You have time, though," she reassured me. I was eighteen years old. I was studying English literature. I had discovered Milton, Shakespeare, Auden, T.S. Eliot, Shelley, Keats and Blake. That may have been what took me to England.

I had really wanted to love London. When I arrived, broke and anxious for work, I thought London put Budapest to shame: this was a great city. I fed pigeons in Trafalgar Square, checked out the stores on King's Road, walked both sides of the Thames, stood in line for student tickets at the galleries, climbed the narrow staircases of the Tower, read history, ate Wimpy burgers, drank G & T's and warm beer in pubs. I read Dickens, Smollett, George Eliot, Virginia Woolf, James Joyce, Thackeray, Hardy, E.M. Forster, Henry James, Christopher Isherwood. I saw my first Shakespeare play and finally understood why *Love's Labour's Lost* is a comedy and *Measure for Measure* is not.

Determined not to wash toilets any more, I lied my way into a job at Cassell. There was just enough pay for a fifth of a basement flat, but at least I was in publishing, and I knew my grandfather would approve. The flat was shared by Kiwis (as New Zealanders called themselves) and Aussies. We took turns in the bathtub, each person's water becoming progressively colder. We couldn't afford more than one tubful of hot water each day.

London was an adventure, not a home. Though I had grown to love their literature, I felt hopelessly foreign amongst the English. When I read George Mikes's *How to Be an Alien*, I knew why.

Visiting London now, I can see myself walking up Kensington Church Street to Notting Hill tube station. By now, I imagine, I have a brown speckled umbrella, and it's opened. I wear a brown mac and have a rolled newspaper under my arm. I gaze at my reflection in the shop windows along Oxford Street; I am still trying to fit in. I catch sight of myself, too, in the Red Lion pub near Marble Arch, where I used to hang out with the salespeople from Collier Macmillan. I am trying to sound English, dyeing my hair purple and wearing black vinyl boots or button-down cardigans and scratchy brown hose, thinking of becoming a writer but travelling too much to write.

When I lived in London, I was always travelling, coming back ready for the next trip. I think even then I was looking for a place where I could stay. I saw most of Scotland, as well as every university town in England, Norway, Sweden and Denmark. I talked with the ghostly friar in Trondheim cathedral, fed the goldfish in the pond of Stockholm's Grand Hotel, fished off a houseboat along the coast, near Lund and got drunk on Polish vodka at the Majestic in Helsinki. I doubt I would have married—never there long enough to get to know anybody.

After London I tried Peru, but the poverty was so intense I couldn't sleep nights, and I almost died of typhus. There was something about the cool marble floors of the mansion in Miraflores that made me homesick for the bug-infested home I had shared with my grandparents and my mother in Budapest. A woman in rags near Machu Picchu offered me her baby, and I was afraid to touch it because it was covered in oozing sores. In the end, I felt so guilty about neither dying of hunger nor being able to stop anyone else from doing so that I had no regrets left over for the lovely man I had gone to visit.

I arrived in Canada at the beginning of winter. I was carrying a New Zealand passport, a British work permit, an American publisher's guarantee of work, a letter of introduction to a Canadian journalist from a British character actor who had distinguished himself playing a Dalek on *Doctor Who*, a blue suitcase with everything I owned, and a sense of foreboding. I checked into the Royal York Hotel in Toronto and studied the wallpaper overnight. A series of green and yellow hunting scenes. Some blue sky. The operator crackled with delight when I asked her to "knock me up in the morning." She'd heard the British expression before, but it hadn't ceased to amuse her.

At 7 A.M. there was no blue sky over Toronto. The trees along Front Street were bare, there was a jagged, gusty wind the doorman said came off the lake, scrunched newspapers flew along the sidewalk. Everything seemed grey. In a small park, on a bench, a man wearing a green army greatcoat offered to share his sandwich with me. "You're gonna be mighty cold in that short dress, young lady."

An Indian woman in a drugstore near University Avenue told me where to buy something to cover my head. "This wind," she said, "is cold enough to make you deaf." She admired my white boots and guessed I had come from England. "You should have come last year for Expo. What an adventure. We had millions of visitors. My parents came all the way from Delhi."

The first person I met in the publisher's office helped me find the apartments-to-share ads in *The Toronto Star* and gave me two pillows, a mattress and sheets. My new boss took me on a bar crawl that included a big old place way up Yonge Street, the Brunswick House on Bloor Street East and, at mid-town, the Barmaid's Arms. "Not enough pubs here for what you're used to, but the bars are grand." He was in his fifties, sturdy, blue-eyed, had been in the navy, played piano, sang ballads and old navy songs. I knew all the words to "Farewell to Nova Scotia" before I found out where Nova Scotia was.

My roommate had been born in Toronto, but her parents were English. She longed to visit "the old country" and loved what she thought was my puffy

English accent. "That's a bit of New Zealand twang now and then, isn't it?" I hadn't mentioned I was Hungarian. In Christchurch, Hungarian meant lousy foreigner; in London, bloody alien, with the hint that one was breathing air meant for the English. I hadn't yet worked out what it meant in Canada.

My letter of introduction produced a sumptuous meal at a King Street eatery and an English journalist who told me he would never live anywhere else but here. He talked about Pierre Trudeau, who was about to become prime minister, and the people at Toronto city hall who were going to give new meaning to "participatory democracy." They planned to stop development at the core of Toronto; they knew what made for a great city, and it wasn't expressways, it was people.

Long before it was summer I had decided this place was warm enough to stay a while. By then I was working for Jack McClelland, Canadian publishing legend, lover of fine writing and Scotch whisky, rakish World War II hero, self-deprecating boy-man with all the charm and enthusiasm of Rhett Butler in his finest moments. He thought I should learn about Canada by reading Canadian writers. Besides, he pointed out, his company was called "The Canadian Publishers," and how the hell would I manage in the editorial department if I knew nothing about the country? "It's the price of admission," he claimed.

I began with Gabrielle Roy, whose strong, isolated heroines spoke of loneliness and betrayal. I went on to Lucy Maud Montgomery and the Anne of Green Gables books, so much less challenging than Roy but pleasant enough, and I determined to go to Prince Edward Island right after I had breathed in the scent of the tall grass on Roy's Prairies. Stephen Leacock proved to be a cheerful if often acerbic companion through the next couple of evenings, then I took off for the Arctic with Farley Mowat and Halifax with Thomas Raddall. I struggled through Frederick Philip Grove, and told Jack I found him plodding and difficult. He suggested I abandon the effort and read Margaret Laurence instead. I had already read *A Jest of God* in England but hadn't known she was Canadian. I stayed up nights reading everything else she had written. Then it was Earle Birney, from "David" to the newest *Selected Poems,* and Irving Layton, Leonard Cohen, Brian Moore, Peter Newman, Pierre Berton.

I discovered Yorkville in its late sixties folk music glory, and Kensington Market, where a Hungarian delicatessen sold Debreceni sausages next to Chinese fruit stores and used clothing boutiques. I hiked the ravines and explored the lakeshore near the Scarborough Bluffs.

Around this time, McClelland and Stewart's editorial department was ghosting a textbook on Canadian history by a well-liked teacher. We had been promised a province-wide book purchase if we submitted the manuscript within two weeks. The problem was, the teacher couldn't write. There were four of us working on creating a manuscript from notes he had produced. My chapters owed considerable credit (unacknowledged to this day) to Pierre Berton, Peter Newman and the most recent addition to my nighttime Canadiana reading, Donald Creighton. "The real Dean of Canadian history," Jack had called him, but I enjoyed Berton's stories much more than Creighton's.

The first Pierre Berton manuscript I read was *The National Dream.* Then I worked backwards through *Klondike* and *The Smug Minority.* In person Berton was intimidating, too large, too solid; he proclaimed rather than talked. But he was thunderously enthusiastic about stories—all-Canadian tales with quirky, wild-eyed heroes and men who believed that just about anything could be done if you put your mind to it.

Then I graduated to *The Apprenticeship of Duddy Kravitz* and *The Incomparable Atuk*. I fell in love with Mordecai Richler. I laughed through most of those novels. "Jack, you didn't tell me Canadian writers were funny!"

"Funny? Wait till you read *Cocksure*—you've just been in London, right?"

In person, Richler was rumpled and grumpy, but I learnt how to sit quietly with him in the Roof Bar of the Park Plaza Hotel, trying to match him drink for drink until he began to talk to me. "Are you sure you want to be in publishing?" he asked. "Can't see why." But when his manuscript for *St. Urbain's Horseman* landed at McClelland and Stewart, he actually asked me what I thought.

I read Margaret Atwood's poetry and her first fiction manuscript, *The Edible Woman*. When I met her, I was amazed at how small and fragile she was for a woman with such a powerful and uncompromising voice. She wore a long skirt made of some thin material and a shawl over her head against the cold. Her editor, Pamela Fry, told me Atwood might read my palm. In a small coffee shop on Yorkville she looked at my hand, but it was too dark to see, she said. Maybe another time. I was quite sure she had seen nothing remarkable and decided to spare me. I was beginning to think that most Canadians were kinder than other people I had met on my travels.

Earle Birney was in his late sixties when he loped into the office demanding to see the young woman Jack McClelland had dared put in charge of his newest book of poems. He was tall, thin, almost gaunt, with sparse white hair, a beard that left his chin naked, and long, strong-fingered hands that grabbed the edge of the desk as he examined my face for signs of trepidation. The truth is I could not be frightened by a man who had written poems ("I call them pomes," he said. "*Poetry* is pretentious.") that ran in circles and squares, that leapt off the edge of the page, formed chairs, buildings, even the Alaska Passage. "It is meant to be spoken. Maybe sung." Pomes shouldn't lie dead on the paper.

Earle had seen the whole country. He spoke of False Creek and the lights over Vancouver, the High Rockies, Newfoundland, Winnipeg and Nova Scotia, and even, lovingly, of Toronto. He talked of Louis Dudek, A.M. Klein, Paul Hiebert (he thought Sarah Binks was fine), Robertson Davies, Ralph Gustafson, Eric Nicol, George Woodcock, and the drunken binges that almost destroyed *Under the*

Volcano. He had travelled the world, written about the Delhi Road, Cuzco, Cartagena, Kyoto, Greece, met Trotsky, survived the war as a rebellious good soldier and turned the experience into his hilarious *Turvey.* "He reminds me," I told Earle, "of the good soldier Schweik." "And so he should," he said. Turvey, Schweik and, later, Hawkeye were cut from the same cloth.

Irving Layton, exuberant, leonine, booming his prophetic warnings at an ever-appreciative world, told me he was born circumcised and might, in time, turn out to be the real Messiah. It was 1970, and he was in love with Aviva and in love with life. He wrote poems he believed would change the world. "Poets err or they lie. / Poems do not give us the truth but / Reveal like lightning the / forked road that leads us to it." My grandfather had said that only poets know the truth; that dictators, if they are smart, imprison poets first because they are the ones who know and can tell.

Irving was the picture-perfect poet. He could see through man-made fog and detect what people really believed. His erotic love poems shocked the prudish. He raged against injustice, anti-Semites, Communists who jailed writers, the Russian empire that had silenced Osip Mandelshtahm, the narrow-minded, the pitiless, the self-righteous, the categorical, the "rat-faced cunning mercers," men whose worlds were built entirely of money, hypocrites, and those who had never read a poem.

He gave me "For Anna," in a restaurant on Yorkville:

You wanted the perfect setting
for your old-world beauty, post-war Hungarian:
a downtown Toronto bar sleazy
with young whores pimps small-time racketeers

Remembering boyhood Xmases in Elmira
plus one poet pissed to the gills
by turns raving like an acidhead
then suddenly silent like the inside of a glass.

I debated with Farley Mowat about his book on Siberia and the true nature of Russian communism, about Stalin's heritage. His *Never Cry Wolf* had become such a trail blazing best-seller in the Soviet Union, he was convinced the system would work, given time and trust. I wasn't. I was afraid to tell him about the young Russian soldier I had watched die in

Budapest, and didn't mention my experiments with firing a machine gun. The sun was too bright that day in Port Hope, and he was too ecstatic about the Russians he had met.

I had already read his *And No Birds Sang*. In 1942, when Farley was barely out of his teens, his regiment fought through the blood-soaked mountains of Italy. There was no time to bury the dead. His war made my revolution look like child's play.

It was Farley who insisted I would never know Canada until I had been to the Arctic.

When Matt Cohen entered my life, I was beginning to feel settled in Toronto. He handed me his manuscript for *Johnny Crackle Sings*, and was stunned that I loved it. He was a gawky young man, around my own age, painfully shy, uncertain of his talent but sure he was already a writer. We drank wine at the Inn on the Park and debated God and Maimonides, German determinism, discussed George Grant's *Lament for a Nation*, Camus, Sartre and his circle of sycophants, and what was the reason for literature. When, at his request, I edited *The Disinherited*, I felt as if I had lived in southern Ontario forever; all his people seemed to be kin.

Later, when I drove through the area north of Kingston, hardscrabble farming land, I recognized Matt's landscape. I thought I saw Richard Thomas striding from an old stone barn towards the gabled farmhouse, and maybe Erik and Brian and, in the distance, running towards the town, Kitty Malone.

I met Al Purdy in front of his house in Ameliasburg. It was early evening, the day turning orange around the trees. I had been sitting in the back of Jack McClelland's Mustang convertible, my knees scrunched under my chin, leaning forward to hear Jack and Harold Town planning how to approach Purdy with the proposition for a new book of love poetry to be illustrated by Harold. Harold was one of Canada's most celebrated and outspoken artists, and Jack's close friend. My role was to be a kind of peacemaker, someone who could bridge the gap between the poet and the artist. It's good to have an outsider for this, Jack suggested; both men have giant egos, both are irascible, but if they can agree to work together, the book will be brilliant. Irving Layton's *Love Where the Nights are Long* had been such a critical success that another such book, this time by Purdy, could not fail.

Al poured drinks—vodka for Jack, Scotch for Harold—and we headed towards the lake. It was a pleasant Ontario fall day, birds getting ready to fly south. The cool air would help us think, or somesuch. Jack wore an Irish knit pullover, Harold had a big batwing cloak he whipped around his shoulders, and Eurithe (Al's very quiet wife) gave me a soft, embroidered shawl. I remember sitting on a tree stump for what seemed like hours while the battle raged between Harold and Al about the relative merits of their contributions to such a book, Harold pacing about in the succulent mud near the lake, Al leaning back on his heels, big hands fisted, like a fighter. Jack swore. I said little.

The argument festered as we marched back to the house. I slept in the loft overlooking the red lantern by whose light they were still arguing, and in the morning, insanely early, we headed off, in silence, to Toronto.

"He is not," Harold asserted when Jack dropped him off at his house near Castle Frank subway station, "a romantic poet."

I disagreed.

"Why in hell didn't you say so earlier?" Jack asked. "Not much sense in your having a point of view now, is there?"

There wasn't. But I hadn't yet acquired the confidence to join in arguments about Canadian poetry.

Al's book was published a couple of years later: *Love in a Burning Building*, some of the most moving love poetry in the world. The book had no drawings by Harold.

My first sight of the Rocky Mountains was on the way to Banff from Calgary. I asked the driver to stop, and walked alongside the car so I could watch the mountains grow, slowly, as we approached. Sure, there had been the Tatras in northern Hungary, and Mount Cook on the South Island of New Zealand; but I had never seen mountains till the Rockies hove into view and grew to their monstrous height around me. They make you understand how insignificant you are. They put your life in perspective. They were also the perfect setting for W.O. Mitchell.

I had read and loved his books during my early marathon tour through Canadian literature. He was now holding court for a small group of creative-writing students in the cafeteria of the Banff School of Fine Arts. He talked as if he had always known them, comfortable, expansive, leaning back long-legged in the too small armchair, telling them about writing in Canada. I thought I had seen most of the country by then, so I decided I'd tell him I had seen it all.

All? He started laughing. You haven't stood on the prairie and known you were the tallest thing for hundreds of miles around, hell, you could pull the whole damn sky down over your head—that's when you know where you belong. When I saw the Prairies, I knew what he meant.

Then I met Margaret Laurence. I think it may have been around the time of her collection of essays called *Heart of a Stranger*. She was warm, hospitable, friendly and intense, wanting to know all about where I had been and what had brought me to Canada. She talked about Africa and about living in isolation both there and in England. She knew how it felt to be out of sync with the world around you, to be a stranger, to try different ways of fitting in. Although she had written eloquently about Africa, she was not of there, wasn't even sure exactly where "there" was. Africa is so vast, so harsh and accepting at the same time. In England she had felt lonely, a stranger, but now, back in Canada, she was not sure of her roots.

We were sitting at her kitchen table. She reached across and put her hand on mine where I had been stubbing out my cigarettes. She said I smoked too

much, that I should give myself leave to relax and settle; that Canada was even more accepting than
Africa, if you allowed it to be.

She had been working on a novel she wasn't sure
she would ever be able to finish. Later, when *The
Diviners* was published, I escorted her around the
grounds near the Science Centre, as we both played
our parts in one of Jack McClelland's nuttier promotion efforts. There was a real water diviner, Margaret
with her own divining branch, and myself with a
mickey of gin, trying vainly to return the favour and
keep her spirits up.

Has anyone ever had such an education in becoming
a citizen?

I am not sure exactly when I knew I belonged, but I
remember hearing a woman at a cocktail party in
Vancouver say that Canada had produced no writers
of international quality. (She may have said "world-
class," though I think that horrendous phrase hadn't
yet made its way into the language.) I was so out-
raged, I yelled at her and the assembled group who
had been listening to her nonsense. I told her she

wouldn't know quality if she tripped over it, and later I called Jack and asked him whether, being Hungarian, a New Zealander and British, I could join his Committee for an Independent Canada.

When my first, all-Canadian daughter was born, Earle Birney wrote her a poem that starts "Welcome, welcome, Catherine Porter . . ." And as she grew, I began to tell her the stories I had learnt along my journey. Who knows, one day she may even go to Hungary alone, or with her sister, and check the galleries for those grim-faced ancestors, visit Kula in Bácska, where my great-grandfather's and great-great-grandfather's graves are marked by a white stone cross in an ancient cemetery, and maybe drive to the remote village of Tövis in Transylvania and seek out where the journey began.

———

Ken Wiwa

—

AN INVENTORY OF BELONGING

I WAS TEN YEARS OLD when I first felt the anxious thrill of moving to another country. My father had decided to send me to school in England. As I took my seat in the aircraft at Lagos airport in Nigeria, I had no idea that I was swapping the security of an idyllic African childhood for the uncertainties of adolescence abroad. I remember staring at my new name in my passport. I'd always been known as Junior, and it wasn't until my father informed me that he was sending me to England that I found out my real name was Kenule. As I took in my "new" name, Kenule Bornale Saro-Wiwa, it looked and felt as flat and lifeless as the page it was printed on. I had no idea that that name would turn out to be a multi-dimensional puzzle that would trouble me, stalking my emerging sense of self so that I would spend the next twenty years of my life trying, consciously and unconsciously, to make an accommodation with this name that my father had given me.

I am an Ogoni, one of the 500,000 people who live on a gently sloping, fertile and oil-rich land. The canvas of our story is Ogoni, the 404 square-mile plateau of the Niger River's flood plains in southern Nigeria. This is where my ancestors have lived since time began, according to one of our many creation myths. The history of the Ogoni people is rich in event, but it wasn't until 1958, when oil was discovered on our lands, that Ogoni was plugged into the global economy. Until then we were mainly subsistence farmers and fishermen who had minimal contact with the outside world. With the advent of the oil companies, however, things changed. For the worse. A resource that should have made Ogoni as rich as a small Gulf state turned out to be a curse.

Gas flared twenty-four hours a day, pumping noxious fumes into the atmosphere and poisoning the rain. Hundreds of miles of rusting pipeline, laid without community consultation, often over farm-land, spilled oil into the soil and the water table, compromising the community's ability to farm and fish our traditional lands and waters. An estimated

900 million barrels of oil worth some $30 billion has been pumped out of Ogoni, and yet the people there have no pipe-borne water, no electricity, no telephone service, very few tarred roads, no hospital worthy of the name and very little in the form of education. In this land of plenty, 70 percent of Ogoni graduates are unemployed.

Our people suffer not only from the predations of international business but from the ethnic chauvinism and discrimination that is rampant in Nigeria. As a minority in a nation of 250 ethnic groups, we were seen by Nigeria's often unelected leaders as dispensable; our people could be displaced and our resources stolen without consultation. They assumed we were too small, that we lacked a coherent and concerted voice with which to speak out against our treatment.

Until 1993, that is. In January of that year, 300,000 Ogonis came out to protest against the discrimination they faced at the hands of Nigeria's government and Shell Oil. That three out of five Ogonis had participated in a peaceful demonstration alarmed both Shell and the military regime, who feared the prospect of such concerted grassroots action spreading among the many oil-bearing communities in the Niger Delta. The government and Shell resolved to intimidate the Ogoni and its leaders into silence.

That so many people had turned out to protest was thanks to MOSOP (Movement for the Survival of the Ogoni People). My father had founded the movement in 1990, and sent its activists out into the community to educate and mobilize grassroots opinion. After a year of arrests and detentions, my father was jailed for what proved to be the final time on April 23, 1994. He was tried on trumped-up murder charges and, despite an international campaign and protests, was hanged on November 10, 1995.

My father's life and death left me to face an ever-present question about the home he had lived and died to protect. It left me thinking: How much do I claim from it and how much does it claim of me?

My father was an anglophile, a passion he developed as a teenager at his secondary school in southern Nigeria. This love of things English has been bred into my family's genes. My great-grandfather started it; he was the one who brought English missionaries to our village. I suspect it was also the reason why his son, my grandfather, Jim Wiwa, has an English name. My father was the first one in the family to receive a formal English education. Through a government scholarship he went "abroad" to Umuahia, a town 125 kilometres from home, where he was one of a handful of Ogoni students. It was at Umuahia that Ken Saro-Wiwa fell in love with all things English. Modelled on an English boarding school, Umuahia was run by expatriate teachers in the colonial service. By the time Ken Saro-Wiwa's first son was ready for secondary school, Nigeria had long since been independent from the British, and the school system we inherited from our former masters had been abused by the ruinous politics of the country. Which was why my father sent me to school in England.

The shock of being yanked out of the security of my African childhood and thrust into adolescence in Europe exerted a profound influence on my emerging identity. Faced with the self-confidence and assumptions of my peers, I began to reinvent my identity to fit my new environment. So Kenule became Ken and I began to speak with the same accent as my English friends, subconsciously absorbing the world view that had enabled a small island nation to exert a disproportionate influence on the world. I floated between the certainties of my childhood in Africa and the twilight world of adolescence in England; as much as I wanted to be like my friends, I knew deep down that I was not one of them. I remember the resentment I felt whenever I watched *Tarzan*. I hated the way the Africans were always shown as faceless, voiceless extras to Johnny Weismuller's tall, blond muscular master of the jungle. I resented the premise of films like *Zulu* with their implicit message of African subservience to the white man. But I also knew that, like Tarzan, I had to be like the natives to survive in the jungle of an English private school.

Twenty years in England moulded my identity. My accent, my values, my world view—so much about me became anglicized. It wasn't until I was twenty-six that I began to question that identity. Until then there had always been this vague, unexplored, uncomfortable and unspeakable feeling of betrayal, a sense of shame at my identification more with European values than with African ones. And so, when my father's political activities in Nigeria demanded that I repay the faith he had invested in me, I obliged him as any dutiful son would, but I was aware that my involvement in my father's politics would have long-term consequences for my identity.

The deeper I was drawn into his world, the more resentful I became that so many of my choices in life had been motivated by a desire to escape his influence rather than by what I actually wanted for myself. After he was murdered, those feelings intensified. I was torn between my now politicized identity as Ken

Saro-Wiwa's son and the apolitical, anglicized identity I had had in England. I was hovering between a
country I had tried to leave behind and now wanted
to forget, and a country that was trying to shoehorn
me into an identity that no longer fitted me. By the
time I was twenty-nine, I had no idea who I was or
what I wanted to be. I had no clear concept of where
home was or to whom or what I owed my allegiance.
I was deracinated, adrift in the world.

Because I was schooled in England, my life was
divided between Africa and Europe, and I floated
between two worlds, following the course that had
been mapped out by my father's love of all things
English and his simultaneous fierce commitment to
our home. While England was fashioning me into an
Englishman, an identity I never felt entirely comfortable with, I was even less at home with my father's
increasingly passionate crusade to preserve the cultural identity of our people in Africa. At school I was
English by default; at home I was a reluctant
Nigerian. The two parts of me were mutually exclu-
sive, but it was my relationship with Father that
exercised the strongest influence on my emerging
identity. As his first son and namesake I became
increasingly aware of the need to make a name for
myself, a name that was distinct from the one I shared

with him—Ken Saro-Wiwa. So it was perhaps inevitable that I would reject Africa, if only as a declaration of my independence from him.

In September 1997, I determined to resolve, once and for all, the competing claims to my identity.

I'd known Mark Johnston from the time we worked together on the campaign to try to save my father's life. Mark had returned to Toronto after my father was murdered, and when I confided to him that I was thinking of writing a book, he put me in touch with Alberto Manguel.

I dashed off a couple of chapters and sent them to Alberto. He was living in London at the time, where he had edited an issue of *Index on Censorship* magazine featuring one of my father's short stories.

"Would you like me to be gentle or tough?" Alberto asked after reading my sample chapters.

"Be tough," I braved.

"Well, this is bullshit," he duly obliged. "When I hear you talk about your father," Alberto explained, "it makes the hairs on the back of my neck stand on end. These chapters don't do that for me," he said, thumbing the manuscript with a fastidious frown on his face.

I went away and had another go, writing and rewriting, trying to pour my anxieties onto the page. I went back to Alberto, and he pointedly put the manuscript aside as he patiently listened to me describe my dilemmas again. When I had finished, he leaned back in his chair and stroked his beard.

"Hmm," he purred. "You haven't found your voice," he mused in his gentle lilting accent.

He suggested I write a letter to my dead father, and I left to look for my voice. In a sense life is all about this struggle to find a distinctive voice to call our own. In our various voices we hear our influences: our parents, our role models, our communities. My problem, in September 1997, was that I just couldn't decide what my authentic voice sounded like. Was I a Nigerian who had been educated in England? Or an Englishman who was born in Nigeria? Was my essence revealed in the middle-class accent and values I had picked up at my boarding schools, or the Nigerian accent and values that spoke up instinctively when I was in the company of my African friends and family? What was my default accent?

I experimented, trying out my different voices, switching personas, chopping and changing, torturing and confusing the poor manuscript. During yet another anguished confession Alberto asked if I liked living in England. I told him I had nothing against the place, but I was concerned that in England my identity was fixed as Ken Saro-Wiwa's son, so people now had preconceptions of who I was or ought to be. And once you are pigeonholed in England, it is tough to convince anyone that you have anything else to offer. I didn't particularly relish the prospect of spending the rest of my life being introduced as Ken Saro-Wiwa's son—especially as I was by then a father myself.

Alberto wanted to know if I'd ever considered moving to Canada. I replied that I'd always had a soft spot for Canadians, especially after the way Canadian writers and the Canadian government had championed my father's cause and spoken out in support of him. I might even have explained that during my first visit to Canada in 1995, when I attended a PEN benefit in honour of my father, I'd had a drunken premonition that I would one day live in Canada. But when Alberto suggested that I consider moving there and told me that the government had a visa program that encouraged writers and artists to come and work in Canada, I recoiled from the idea. I couldn't imagine upping sticks to a country I barely knew.

Over the course of the next year the idea grew on me. The more I struggled to find my voice, the more

I came to appreciate that a change of scene might help. So I began to reconsider—especially as I kept running into Canada's growing literary profile. And the more I heard that this was due to Canada's openness to writers from all over the world, the more attractive the Canadian option became.

I am watching my son sleeping. Somewhere in the corridors of my memory I can hear the words from a television documentary about the lions of the Serengeti.

When the cubs are old enough to fend for themselves, the stentorian voice of the disembodied narrator is explaining, *their parents will chase them away and into the wild, where the young lions will roam until they are ready to settle down and establish a pride of their own. When it is ready to die, a lion will trek for miles across the parched Serengeti to the exact spot where it was born.*

The memory of these words triggers an old, recurring pang of guilt. My father sent me abroad so that I would return home one day and apply my expensively trained mind to the problems facing our people. But here I am in Canada, as far away from Africa as he could possibly have feared—and this after all the financial and emotional expense of my education, and after my father has been murdered for trying to protect the idea and sanctity of our home and community. As the familiar feelings of betrayal well up, I find myself reflecting on those lions of the Serengeti. Whenever the past gnaws at my conscience, I try to calm myself with the thought that we are all lions on the Serengeti. Each of us, at some point in his life, has to leave home to establish his pride, to find a place of his own. Which, when you think it through, means that a lion never dies in the same place as its progeny.

I sometimes wonder, as I stare out of this window, at the U-turns, chance meetings, reckless gambles and inspired decisions on which our lives turn. Do we actively make choices or are we passive objects of the choices that fate imposes? Was it really some unconscious desire to return to Africa that sent me on this grand detour? Because of course the irony is that when I am in this room, I actually feel closer to home, to Africa, than I have ever done since I left.

I knew, the minute I set eyes on this room, that I wanted to live in this house. It is a small room, maybe ten by six, an annex of my bedroom. I say "I knew," but it was as much an unconscious as a conscious decision. So many of the choices we make in life are informed by our past, and I strongly suspect that my wish to live in this particular house was inspired by summer holidays spent loitering in my father's study in an annex of *his* bedroom in Nigeria. I would scan the shelves of his library, plucking out any book that caught my wayward fancy, dipping in and out of its pages, reading indiscriminately—Swift, Shakespeare, Dickens, Sir Arthur Conan Doyle. Flitting from Soyinka to Senghor, between Achebe and Pepper Clarke, I would search for something to help while away the holiday until it was time to return to school in England.

The books on the shelves in here are familiar. I too have accumulated a library featuring Chinua Achebe, Wole Soyinka and John Pepper Clarke. I also have two books by the grand old man of African letters, the former Senegalese poet, soldier, priest and president Leopold Sedar Senghor. Monsieur Senghor was my father's ideal of the Renaissance man, *l'homme engagé,* as Ken Saro-Wiwa liked to envisage himself. I've never actually read Senghor, but I bought his books anyway. I am conscious that this room is something of a shrine to my father, that it reflects an unconscious need to belong, to establish a connection with him and with *that* faraway home.

When I look around at the mess in here—the jumble of books, newspapers, passports, compact discs and photographs—I see a pattern in the rug. I see the outline of my face, I hear the sound of a voice, barely audible, like a faint whisper carried on the wind. Take, for instance, the books on my shelves. They are not arranged in any particular order, but I know instinctively where to find every title. There is a method to this madness, because those books didn't get where they are by accident. I remember why I bought each one, why and when I placed it, seemingly at random, on the shelves.

When I left England, I had to prune my library. I had far too many books, and I decided to leave behind the ones that had helped construct the identity I was no longer comfortable with. I spent hours trying to decide which books to take and which to leave behind, yet I still ended up shipping a hundred titles over. Books are deceptively heavy and these ones cost me far more than I could afford; but I brought them anyway, because I knew I was moving to a country that encourages you to bring your past with you. Even the books that have been added since I arrived here have a recurring theme: the quest for personal identity against the foreground of politics and the recurring echoes of history. You get a generous baggage allowance when you move to Canada.

There are two books in here that I carry around

with me wherever I travel. They contain a log of all the journeys I have made since 1995. My two passports record some of the places I travelled on my father's behalf: New Zealand, Canada and the U.S., Germany, Austria, France, Belgium, Ireland. I went to all these places in an effort to save his life. Even after he was killed, I carried on travelling, trying to understand what his life and death would mean to me. I went to Burma, to South Africa, back to Canada again, and finally to Nigeria to bury him last year. I still travel a lot—sometimes on his behalf but increasingly on mine. But wherever I roam, all roads lead back to Canada.

My passports also tell another story. In my Nigerian passport I am identified as Kenule Bornale Saro-Wiwa. In my British passport I am listed as Saro Kenule Bornale Wiwa. The official who issued my Nigerian passport last year informed me, somewhat gleefully, that he had to use the name that was on my previous Nigerian passport. So even though I had legally changed my name in 1993, the Saro-Wiwa name lives on in Nigeria. I will soon be eligible for Canadian citizenship and I toy with the notion of reclaiming the name if I apply for a Canadian passport. It's only a fleeting thought, though, because the short answer to the question "Why Canada?" is that

I came here to discover and define who Ken Wiwa is. Canada, as it promised, has given me the space to reinvent or at least discover myself, and I now have a clearer sense of who this Ken Wiwa is and to whom and what the fellow owes his allegiance. That said, I am also aware that deep down there will always be a Ken Saro-Wiwa in me.

I often shrink from the realization that so much of my writing is self-centred. But I also suffer from the delusion that my experience reflects a wider, more universal, or at least Canadian concern. The world is shrinking so quickly, people are moving around so much, mingling and intermarrying, that we keep being told we now live in a world without frontiers— a global village. But I sometimes wonder whether it won't be more important than ever to root ourselves in something, to identify with somewhere specific. We still need to fix our values in a coherent system, to believe in something—an idea, a community of shared aspirations perhaps. We have to lay down a default identity that we can turn to and cling to in times of confusion and bewildering events. As James Baldwin once surmised, too much identity is a bad thing, but too little can also be a problem.

I imagine that's why the only shelf in my library that displays any semblance of order is the one devoted to my father's books and letters. My father roots me, reminds me of the place I came from. He is my default template, the clay from which I mould my image. And now that I have defined him, quantified his values and made sense of the questions he once posed to my sense of self, I can begin to look for my own answers. When I am in here, I feel reassured that he is close at hand, that I can reach over and reread his words, look between the lines, talk to him, engage in a debate with him. When I am in here, I am in my father's study. I am also back in Africa. And I am in Canada. I am at home.

As I sit here typing these words, writing into the future, I am conscious of the folder that sits on the shelf with my father's books. In that folder is a letter my father sent me from his detention cell. It was one of the last letters he wrote to me, and it contains the most important advice my father ever gave me:

I don't mind you growing your children outside . . . you should use the advantages which your British experience has offered you to promote your African/Ogoniness . . .

Those words have become my mission statement in life. They define and sustain me in my quest to fulfill my obligations to myself, my family, my father and my community. If Ken Saro-Wiwa had known how things would turn out for his first son, he probably would have substituted *Canadian* for *British* in that letter, because it is here, in Canada, that I found the space from which to express myself and begin the quest to promote my home.

———

Brian D. Johnson

—

FROM THE LIGHTHOUSE

I NEVER USED TO think of myself as an immigrant. Not until my wife, who is Canadian-born, played the birthright card during an argument we were having about national unity during the last Quebec referendum. "But of course," she said, "you're not *from* here."

I still have trouble calling myself an immigrant without some irony. We associate immigrants with the colonized and the dispossessed, whereas I came from the so-called Mother Country, home to the colonizers and the self-possessed. My family moved here, not to escape hardship or repression, but because an executive post opened up for my father at the Canadian branch of an English insurance company called the Pearl—the Pearl *Ass*urance Company, which had a more comforting ring than *in*surance. For us, it would always be the Mother Company, mother of pearl, cradle to grave. I'd lived just five years in England before emigrating. But it would take much longer to feel released from the embrace of empire, with all its cozy intonations of class and race and gender. When we moved to Canada, England moved with us. And I wouldn't shake myself free of it until my mid-twenties, when I "emigrated" a second time, from English Canada to Quebec. There, in a quicksilver romance with another culture, in the bright shock of difference, I caught a new reflection of myself—at home in my own skin—and finally left England behind.

Since then I think I've come to understand that immigration is not just about changing countries. You can cross four thousand miles of ocean from England to Canada and not feel like an immigrant; or you can move five hours down the road from one piece of Canada to another and make yourself strangely at home in a foreign culture. Then there's the country of the mind, where the frontiers are elusive, forever shifting.

My early childhood memories amount to a handful of sensory images. I grew up in a seaside town called Whitley Bay, near Newcastle upon Tyne. We lived on Queen's Road, which ended in a field where horses licked sugar cubes out of my hand, and beyond that were out-of-bounds brambles and railway tracks.

I remember making mud balls by a coal fire in winter. Summer weekends on a cold beach, knees turning blue in the icy shriek of the North Sea. Eating potato crisps from a bag that came with its own little pack of salt that got mixed up with the sand on my fingers. When the tide was out, we'd walk to the lighthouse. Out and back. That smooth white tower was Whitley Bay's postcard landmark.

On the other side of town was the Spanish City, a carnival midway greased with danger and dark skin. It was the most foreign place imaginable. I never went there but always heard it talked about as a forbidden zone, a cartoon example of what it meant to be "common." Years later, in Canada, whenever the family would drive along a country road and ride over those sudden hills that make you feel briefly airborne, we'd shout "Spanish City bumps!" in a happy chorus. It was a reference to the roller coaster in that Whitley Bay fairground, but the phrase had become so familiar to me that I'd forgotten its origin, assuming it was just an English idiom for a hilly road.

When I left England at the age of five I was too young to know what a country was, never mind a "Canada." I was under the impression that we were taking a ship to see a cannon. Ship, cannon—there was a certain logic to it. And I still remember the disappointment of walking down vast white gangway corridors into an indoor ship that didn't look like a ship, and then being told, amid much laughter, that there would be no cannon, only this place called Canada. It was October 1954, and we were sailing on the *Empress of France*—my mother, my ten-year-old brother and myself. My father had gone ahead by plane to buy a house.

It was a rough crossing. In the mid-Atlantic we were whiplashed by the tail end of Hurricane Hazel, a monster storm that was a step ahead of us, also en route to Toronto but travelling at a faster clip. We spent most of the passage lying seasick below decks, being served Canada Dry ginger ale by a kindly cabin steward. For my mother the whole experience was terrifying. She'd never been on a ship or a plane, and hadn't ventured farther from home than the Devon coast. Now she was travelling alone, sailing into an uncertain future with two small children. On the ship, we met the Chilcotts, a couple immigrating to Toronto because of another branch-office job at an English insurance company. It's as if the insurance men were the last missionaries, out to civilize a precarious future. The Chilcotts became our good friends. In our new home, where we had no relatives, we'd spend every Christmas with them, keeping alive the English tradition of turkey with stuffing balls, bread sauce and sherry trifle.

Although the passage was rough, we weren't exactly boat people. We spent out first three weeks at the Royal York Hotel, experiencing a comfy form of culture shock. After reaching Toronto, we couldn't get to our new house because Hurricane Hazel had washed out the bridges to the west end. (Hazel was the worst natural disaster in Canadian history. Eighty-one people were killed in Toronto, thirty-two of them when a row of fourteen houses slid into the Humber River.)

In the New World everything looked huge—the streets, the cars, the buildings, the steaks. My brother and I spent our days tearing up and down the mammoth corridors of the Royal York, which was the biggest building we'd ever seen, the centrepiece of a skyline that was immeasurably tall and modern. Boys love bigness, and Canada was larger than life.

We moved to a bungalow on the suburban frontier, an Etobicoke subdivision still scarred and muddy from the storm. The wildness of the country was just a short walk away, across the field and through the woods to the creek and Snapping Turtle Pond. My father spent weekends sinking fence posts around the treeless yard, and panelling the rec room. He finished just in time to sell the house and buy a better one, where he panelled another rec room. My brother and I hung plastic models of American warplanes on the fresh walls, and played ping-pong to pancake stacks of 45s. Ray Charles, Del Shannon, Duane Eddy, Chuck Berry. The novelties of growing up—music, TV and toys—were American, but the rest of Canada was as British as it was Canadian. So we fit right in. It was the early sixties. There was no flag, no Margaret Atwood, no Gordon Lightfoot or Joni Mitchell. Aside from the black-and-white beauty of *Hockey Night in Canada*, a ritual our whole family happily embraced, Canadian identity was barely an idea. But everywhere you looked, there were signs of the Motherland, from ubiquitous reminders of the Queen to the home-country twang of Ray Sonin hosting *Calling All Britons* on CFRB radio.

We were not rich. My father worked so hard to create a comfortable life for us that he didn't live long enough to fully reap the benefits. His own father had died when he was a boy, so he gave up a dream of becoming an engineer and went to work to support his mother. He always had a healthy respect for money. He would keep coins stacked in perfect little towers on his dresser. A man of routine. He once told me, with a grin of immense satisfaction, that he always put his socks on first when he got dressed in the morning. Although he never offered an explanation, it always struck me as a precaution against something. As an insurance man, Father believed in guarding against calamity.

My parents arrived in Canada with some notions of class that were not about money. They couldn't get used to the idea of seeing my older brother and me heading off to school in jeans. They worried about us falling in with the wrong crowd, the kind of kids their own parents would have called "common." So they scrimped and saved to send us both to Upper Canada College, an uncommonly private school, where I would spend ten years. Upper Canada was an ersatz England, with masters instead of teachers, forms instead of grades. The cane, not the strap, was the scourge of choice. We played cricket in the spring. And there were more than a few English accents among the faculty.

My most formative teacher was a Brit who got me addicted to reading books. He fed me true stories of the Second World War, and by the time I was twelve, I'd read them all: fighter ace Douglas Bader gunning down Germans in the Battle of Britain after losing both his legs, the Dambusters sneaking bombs down rivers, wounded men on morphine skiing to freedom in Scandinavia, frozen sailors manning convoys to Murmansk, the silent dread of the U-boat wolf packs, the bomber crews haunted by the sweet odour of human flesh burning in the incendiary attacks on Hamburg and Dresden, and all those nifty British aircraft—Spitfires, Hurricanes, Lancasters, Mosquitoes. In the late fifties the war was still in the relatively recent past, and its literature had blossomed. It was, I think, the reason I became a writer. I wanted to emulate what I'd read, and even attempted a bogus short story of escaping from a prison camp and waiting to feel the thud of bullets in my back.

Because I didn't board at Upper Canada, I was spared the habitual canings and pedophile intrigues that were the price of living on the grounds. But unlike other "day boys," many of whom lived nearby in opulent Forest Hill, I commuted ten miles each day from Etobicoke, and that fostered a split personality of sorts. My life contained two distinct worlds: a private school of ties and blazers and Anglican hymns, and a suburb of Popsicles, bikes and creeks. Torn between school and suburb, I felt like an imposter in both, never rich or cool enough to fit into cliquish Upper Canada, and a stranger to the ordinary life of suburban kids who wore jeans and knew girls. Between these two worlds was my father's car radio, tuned to early rock'n'roll exactly half the time (he was scrupulously fair). This was the sound of America, pre-Beatles, and for my brother and me it was the first thing that felt truly ours. Elvis separated us from our parents, and from England, unequivocally. My mother was no square— she always liked "a good beat" and loved to dance—but she couldn't stand the grease or the sneer. Elvis *was* the Spanish City.

Meanwhile, another kind of rift had opened in my psyche. Soon after arriving in Canada, I remember playing with some neighbourhood kids in the dirt of a cinder-block foundation and being teased about my English accent. From then on I worked to eliminate it. At home, however, I maintained my cover. The crucial test came around words like "pyjama" and "banana," with vowels that couldn't be fudged. It's not that my parents enforced the accent; they were always tolerant and eager to adapt. But at the time, speaking "Canadian" felt oddly sinful. Our family was never religious. God, like sex, was a subject not raised in polite company. The only thing resembling religion was our Englishness, an unspoken creed that prized a modest sense of superiority. It was good to have money, but not to flaunt it. Politeness was proof of good breeding. And excess of any kind was suspicious;

sweets must not be too sweet or meat too well done, and large California strawberries were a reminder that fruit and vegetables had more taste "back home."

Food, of course, is central to any culture, and my mother's cooking provided the most tangible link to the place that she and my father still called "home" two decades after emigrating. English cooking gets a bad rap for being tasteless and overcooked, but I have only good memories of my mother's cuisine: steak-and-kidney pie with a hard-boiled egg, Atlantic-white flakes of milk-poached fin-and-haddie, roast-beef gravy poured into crispy towers of Yorkshire pudding. This was comfort food, and *pudding* was the operative word. Mother's desserts shaped my sybaritic nature from an early age. I was forever spoiled by her un-American apple pie, sugared just past the edge of tartness. And so many puddings—steamed pudding in rivers of warm custard, bread pudding milk-sweet and soft, rice pudding with its tawny skin, the meringue loft of Queen's pudding layered with raspberry jam, the pillowy depths of blancmange, the infamous Christmas trifle booby-trapped with liquor—not to mention the family-heirloom fruitcake, which was called Georgian Margaret for reasons no one can recall.

For all its comforts, however, in cultural terms an English upbringing was a restricted diet. Other races were, at best, a curiosity. And Upper Canada College was then almost exclusively WASP, male and affluent. Our principal reminded us at every opportunity that we were being groomed to be "leaders." What gave us this privilege was never explained. But one of the things about living among the sons of the ruling class is that you become immune to its charms. The really rich kids were often the most moronic. So I developed a casual contempt for money. By working as journalist, and for several years as a musician, I managed to avoid the wealth I had been trained to expect with *noblesse oblige*. And to this day, although I've developed a desire for money, I remain unimpressed by it.

Attending Upper Canada College was like being the citizen of a small, privileged principality, a city state utterly aloof from the world outside the grounds. And the culture shock of leaving UCC was profound. At the University of Toronto, I enrolled at University College, where the majority of students were Jewish. At the time I'm not sure I knew what it meant to be Jewish, because the more noticeable difference in my environment was that, after ten years, I was finally among female students—*girls* sitting right next to me. I couldn't believe it. Everyone else seemed to take it for granted.

It was the late sixties. I would discover Jews, sex, drugs, rock'n'roll and communism. All at once: listening to Jim Morrison sing "Break on Through to the Other Side" while I made out on the grass of Varsity Stadium, on grass, with Barbara, a Jew who found it amusing that I wasn't Jewish—Barbara who selected me, moved in with me, taught me the beauty of constant fucking, and left me six months later after I went home for Christmas without her. She'd said she didn't mind not coming with me and, like an idiot, I'd believed her.

Christmas was always sacred. But otherwise I lost track of England. In the righteous carnival of radical politics, I turned against my upbringing, my class background and—regrettably—my family. Our generation didn't need a heritage; we were inventing our own. Bastard children of Marx and Freud, we imagined a world ungoverned by family or state, and found a place in the sun of psychedelic drugs, believing in nothing so much as the inarguable beauty of our youth.

Still, one had to work. And for me, like my father, an accident of employment set my destiny. In 1971, after I'd apprenticed as a summer reporter at the Toronto *Telegram*, the newspaper folded. The city editor took me and a few of his young proteges to the

Gazette in Montreal. I thought I was just getting a job, but in moving to Quebec, I became an immigrant once again, rubbing up against a culture that felt thrillingly foreign yet warm and welcoming. In Toronto, I had never once felt foreign; I'd melted into English Canada like a snowflake hitting warm pavement. But in Montreal, the difference was tangible. Embedded in the city's geography, the two solitudes gave explicit form to my own sense of divided identity, which until then had felt internal, more of a dissociated mental state than a cultural condition. In Montreal there was clear demarcation between English and French, or as I saw it at the time, between outside and inside. Here was an opportunity to become truly *déraciné*. Like those English madmen searching out the heat of the noonday sun, I would fling myself into the world until I was as far from home as possible. But in Quebec, I would also feel my first real affection for a national culture, the first kiss of collectivity. I would adopt Quebec as a surrogate mother country, in the secret belief that Quebec had adopted me.

I arrived as a radical journalist incubated by the New Left. After several years of campus politics, supporting struggles that were always happening elsewhere, it was like going into the field. With the most radicalized labour movement on the continent, Quebec was becoming a test tube of class war, a combustible mix of socialism and separatism. And I was infatuated, an Anglo yearning to go native. Everything sounded better in French, especially politics. The language of European Marxism, with words like *débordement* and *petite bourgeoisie,* had the harpsichord ring of high science. And I developed an ear for the funky slur of *joual,* the no-nonsense voice of our much-vaunted *classe ouvrière.*

Learning a language as an adult turns you back into a child at the grown-ups' table. Struggling to decipher conversation above the din of a bar, you look for openings. You rely on innocence and charm to get by, hoping that your blunders will be amusing. Rock-hopping from one familiar piece of vocabulary to the next, you learn to say what you can, not what you want, uttering whatever words come to mind until they form sentences. Now I speak French quite well, but I still find I'm a different person when I do so, someone younger and more naïve—more intuitive, even though French is considered a more rational tongue than English.

The first time I really *got* French—that is, felt the language originate from inside of me—was listening to singer Robert Charlebois, Quebec's original rock star. There's something about music that lets you in. You process the words with a different part of the brain. And at the concerts of Charlebois, Pauline Julien and Louise Forestier, I could melt into the embrace of this foreign culture until there was no line left between it and me. I'd felt the energy of a crowd at plenty of rock concerts, but this was different. There was a sense of articulate collectivity—perhaps not far removed from the parish harmony of a Catholic peasantry. Yet there was nothing provincial about it. It wasn't about anthems or flags. The music was inflected with a transcendent whimsy. Charlebois, who fused rock'n'roll with the Latin rhythms of *joual,* was Quebec's Dylan, Elvis and Jagger all in one. But he invested his "I'm a frog" status as a *beau/laid* icon with enough irony to deflect facile nationalism. When he sang of *trois Amériques en unison,* you imagined a kind of stratospheric parfait, something far more exotic than the club sandwich of sovereignty-association proposed by the PQ.

To be in Quebec in the early seventies was like being in on the continent's best-kept secret. Patronized by France and misunderstood by English North America, it was a unique culture, freshly awoken from generations of Catholic repression by the Quiet Revolution. It was a world of art, music and politics that combined the sophistication of Europe with the energy of America, and the only place you could appreciate it was from the inside, in French. So my infatuation with Quebec culture wasn't groundless. At the same time, however, it was part of a romance with the Other.

In Montreal, whatever double identity I'd developed as an English immigrant in Canada became wildly exaggerated. I lived between two worlds. At *The Gazette*, I became the labour reporter. (That quaint job description has since disappeared, absorbed by the rubric of "business" reporting. But at the time, after a general strike in the public sector, the jailing of the province's top union leaders, and a wave of illegal walkouts and occupations, labour militancy had become *the* major threat to political stability in Quebec, and the best story in town.) While dutifully reporting on the class war for Anglo Montreal's establishment paper, I also worked, anonymously, with a band of Marxist revolutionaries (nothing involving terrorism, in case anyone from csis is listening). I saw myself as a kind of spy, commuting back and forth across class lines. And I developed an irresistible urge to declare my true allegiance, *to go over to the other side*. I meant that in every sense—not just to quit the "bourgeois press," but to go from being observer to actor, and embrace *la patrie imaginaire* of a country not yet invented.

In other words, I was a nervous breakdown waiting to happen. A fault line was opening up in my psyche, which ultimately cracked under the pressure of a political crisis. It's a complicated story, and I was an unreliable witness, so I'll spare you the details. Let's just say that I staged my resignation from *The Gazette* at a press conference. I went quite mad, and fled to Europe, where my lunacy burnt itself out in the volcanic islands of southern Italy. Back in Montreal, I became enchanted with an African drum group led by a Québécois and a Haitian. Whatever inhibiting mechanism in the brain prevents people from succumbing to outlandish desires seemed to have dissolved in mine. I studied voodoo drumming from the Haitian, dropped out of journalism, and returned to Toronto to join a band led by a singer who had just stolen my girlfriend.

I realize this resumé is getting a little wacky, and I won't take you through our Spinal Tap adventures on the road to ever-elusive rock stardom. Suffice it to say that eventually the band broke up, and I re-entered journalism. But touring as a musician involved another kind of emigration. Those years of playing small-town bars—working with my hands— were as close as I'd ever come to the working class I'd spent so much time talking about. Finally, I was *déclassé*; I had calluses. We played Up North and Down East, drinking all night with strangers in corners of Canada I would never have set foot in otherwise. Doing drugs with odd names. Playing a biker bar and hearing the crack of a pool cue across someone's head above the din of the band.

It was a dubious career, and one that couldn't last. But at the time, playing music seemed the most honest way imaginable to make a living. Playing music is the essence of being *inside*. And making art is the ultimate repatriation of self. So even now, when I write about performance as a critic—a professional observer—I try to remind myself what it's like to be on the inside looking out. The immigrant is someone who, by definition, is on the outside looking in, someone whose trip really begins *after* he arrives. And perhaps, through this circuitous passage—immigrating from one Canada to another and back—I had finally landed.

In writing down the circumstances of a life, trying to connect the dots, you wonder what any of it has to do with anything. You want a life to add up, like a work of fiction. But what I've realized in trying to relate my rite of passage is that it's ongoing—and that may say something about the nature of this place. Canada is elusive. It's a shape-shifting country, a trickster nation that keeps forcing us to look inward to understand who we are. Yet for a long time I persisted in looking for answers elsewhere, anywhere but here.

I have no family in Canada aside from my mother, wife and son. My brother lives in Oslo. My mother lives alone in the house where I grew up. There, the faces of my father's ancestors adorn the dining-room wall, as a gallery of gilt-framed miniatures dating back to a certain Edward Johnson in 1694. Photocopied evidence of my mother's Danish heritage recently arrived in the mail, sent by her brother. I learned that my great-uncle, Odin Rosenvinge, made his living painting Cunard ocean liners for postcards—ships that were the forerunners of the one that brought me to Canada. The documents also included a chart from the *Yearbook of Danish Nobility*, which traces my mother's family back to royal roots in Denmark. My heritage, which I have tried so hard to escape, is beginning to look more exotic. Maybe I'm not English after all. For a moment

I entertained the notion that I could be related to Hamlet, which might explain the touch of madness.

On some level, we all emigrate in search of who we are. With or without a ship. Even if we never leave the country, we leave the family to create our own world. Then, at a certain point, when our past begins to loom as mysterious and undiscovered as any place on earth, we try to find our way back before it's too late.

———

Ying Chen

—

ON THE VERGE OF DISAPPEARANCE
(END OF THE CHINESE LETTERS)

DEAR FRIEND,

Your letter, coming from so far away, and after such a long silence, first brought me joy, then troubled me, even more so because I'm in the habit of granting the greatest attention to your feelings and opinions.

I'm glad that even while successfully managing your affairs, you have found the time to read and reread the words of Kong Zi. The two activities should be very complementary, the link between them being so fragile.

You believe that those who don't read Kong Zi are not real Chinese. You seem to be worrying yourself about the moral education of my children, who weren't born in the land of their ancestors. You imagine them in the company of robots, efficient but without souls. I remember, in times past, you weren't preoccupied with moral questions. But now you treat us differently because we're in the West and we run the risk, more than you, of sinking into decadence. I don't know what to say about this. I have the exact same feeling of powerlessness each time a Westerner comments loud and clear about continental China's political system. I don't think a foreign country should be judged according to second-hand information. We can't form a sensible opinion as long as a country and its people are strangers to us, when we don't deign to learn their language, and when we haven't shed sweat and tears on their land.

Don't worry: my descendants born into this land won't be particularly demoralized. I admit that my children won't read the words of Kong Zi (who is here called Confucius) right away. They don't have to learn the science of governing or the necessity of obeying at their young age. They also don't know the Bible yet, which has caused so many torrents of blood to flow. But already they can recite many ancient Chinese poems, and they watch the film *The Little Prince* every day. *The Little Prince* is an excellent moral lesson, accessible to the children and also to me. It portrays the principle of Love, as in all the holy books, but this work has a tenderness and sensitivity without equal, it teaches nothing but the art of living, it questions without resolving. It pleases me because a child is at the centre of the story, and not a sovereign.

You regret the fact that after the Cultural Revolution a new elite left China. You consider this departure one more betrayal of the great tradition. You compare this gesture to the May Fourth Movement at the beginning of the century; you judge them both to be ill-omened. You don't even distinguish the escape and disenchantment of the eighties from the madness of the sixties. You don't untangle the causes from the effects. You prefer the fighters to the escapees. "Once gone," you say, "this elite is quickly Westernized." As you aren't very objective in matters concerning me, it seems, you didn't know to exclude me from this elite. And no one is unaware of the profoundly derogative meaning of the term "Westernized," and the haughty tone of anyone who pronounces it. I left, therefore I'm Westernized, eliminated, lost, disappeared, finished. This is the fate reserved for traitors throughout history.

To save myself from this situation, to elevate myself a bit, you have proposed a solution. You want me to be a double ambassador. You're sure I'm not really a citizen of any place, so you wouldn't hesitate to condemn me to eternal comings and goings. What

I am on the inside is of little importance to you. The individual doesn't count in Kong Zi's book. You think my role is to represent. You want me to live for something bigger than myself. You don't want me as an individual to exist.

Many Westerners would agree with you: a "Westernized" Oriental doesn't have the same charm or value. The West, just like the Orient, can at most tolerate the Other, but has no use for the transformed, the horrific by-products of globalization. (The subject is very hot right now, as though globalization were an event, as though it hasn't been, since the dawn of time, a natural law, an inevitable process in the world's evolution.) The linguistically transformed are sometimes the exception in a given political context. The "politically correct" is only "politically expedient." It creates discontent without changing reality. And political correctness certainly doesn't improve the fate of those in my condition. The sparks and flames of our vestigial selves, which in the end the "politically incorrect" can't put out, will be finished off by the "politically correct" making them banal and ridiculous. The work of xenophobia is often completed by tolerance.

You see, even without crossing the boundaries, without knowing the others' language, your thinking agrees strangely with that of the strangers. Thought is surprisingly uniform; even spatial distance can't change it. The human species, wherever it is found, likes difference. Today we hear, in absolutely every corner of the earth, this same speech: "We're different. Our language is particularly beautiful. Our culture is uncommonly rich and distinguished. Our nation is perpetually menaced with disappearance . . ." And, "Let's live together with our differences." This means living in your own corner, staying in your culture of origin, protecting your spiritual, if not geographic, territory, contenting yourself with appreciating "the other" from a distance. This love of difference is not only in style everywhere, but it's becoming a veritable world tradition. We tried in vain to divide the world into two, or even many, camps. The planet's map is different depending on the angle from which it's seen. But the planet stays the way it is. The world is globalized anyway.

What hit me the hardest in your letter, what provoked a buzzing in my ears, is an allusion that you make to territory. You have qualified me as a "Ji Ju Zhe" in the country where I am. This Chinese expression is an excellent example of the disarming efficiency of my mother tongue. It stuns with sobriety, like a blow from a hammer. My understanding of

Chinese is still good enough for me to suffer fully. A "Ji Ju Zhe" is someone who lives shamefully, pitifully, in a way that's always temporary, under the roofs of others, sheltered from the lights, surviving on the leftovers from others' meals, without contributing anything, like a rodent. (A certain Frenchman named Le Pen would adore this expression. And he's not the only one.) Your letter hits home because it touches an aspect of reality.

When the plane was taking off from the Shanghai airport—twelve years ago already!—I said to myself: it is as if I am dead; I will start everything again elsewhere. I didn't have any intention or need to navigate. I was simply looking for a haven. No battlefield, no ancient ruins, no site under construction, but a garden. Where I was born and grew up, there reigns a mixture of ancient and modern dust that disconcerts me and sometimes makes me suffocate. So I left. To clean out my lungs.

Even if I have never felt compelled, at any moment in my life, to pace off my territory (Kong Zi taught me despite myself to scorn that activity, calculations being, according to him, restrictive to the spirit), I don't like departures and trips. I have always wanted a haven, a routine. All that is familiar to me touches me, holds me. Nobody today believes

in my profoundly sedentary temperament. I'm
always expressing my repugnance towards roots
and my admiration for birds. I praise them for the
freedom that I don't possess. I have lost my wings,
after having lived so long among the ruins. When I
left China, I was no longer a young shoot that could
transplant itself easily. I have neither the courage nor
the force of a real nomad. If I went through another
replanting, I think I would die.

So I don't try to content myself with a voyage.
I aspire to a destiny—a destiny with roots. I like
North America. I say it without blushing. I like this
northern continent (my body doesn't tolerate
extreme heat) for absolutely childish and capricious
reasons that hardly seem to justify the gesture of
uprooting myself. Here, at least, the land is still green
and the sky blue. Do your children know this, a blue
sky? And the moon is disproportionately large, the
way it's seen in drawings. The sidewalks are very
clean. Nowhere else have I seen so many smiling
faces. Here, we rarely have to line up. And we don't
fly into a rage for nothing. It's important. We're calm
when others are calm. One must at least maintain the
appearance of calmness; a little politeness is needed,
some distance, in order to share the planet without
colliding with each other. This appears to be very

Confucianist, very "politically correct." Kong Zi's ambition was to correct our nature, to suppress our instincts. It's what makes him detestable, and also eternal, for our nature doesn't change.

Here live a so-called uprooted people. They no longer recognize it, having quickly fenced in their land, but the others know it. Those from older continents don't forget the matter of age. When the future is uncertain, the past serves as a map. I'm glad to find myself among those who can't look back, who are thrown into the unchartable present. Are you even able to tell who are the real natives here? In the beginning there was desert, like Shanghai one hundred years ago. And the archaeologists tell us that two thousand years is but the blink of an eye. Two thousand years of civilization, a shooting star. And how long will I remain on this earth? Why should I give myself so many worries, ask myself which land belongs to whom? The answer is—the children. My little ones keep me from sleeping serenely. They carry my genes, they're visible. They'll be asked the question: but where do you come from? I already see a shadow covering their young faces; I sense their disarray. And I feel responsible.

Canada is Bethune's country. (But don't believe that Bethune *represents* this country. Nobody, no matter how grandiose his or her destiny, can ever represent anything.) You would be surprised to know that he's almost unknown here. A modest statue in downtown Montreal and a film about him, that's all. Yet he's not only a Chinese hero; he didn't only save the lives of Chinese soldiers, those who very often found themselves under fire not for some ideal or other but simply because they were trying to obtain something to eat and to wear, in exchange for their young blood. Bethune also worked for his compatriots. He fought in concrete terms for universal health care, for one of the best systems in the world in his era, even better now (despite the current problems), better than in China in any case; for which the Canadians rejoice while complaining, and which those without papers dream of while dying in the boats. But Bethune is gone. On the other side of the ocean, a quarter of the human population knows him; in his native country, he has disappeared. There are some who believe he committed suicide, or that he was suicidal in throwing himself into the vast Orient.

As though to mark the end of my wandering, according to custom, I went to sing a solemn tune in front of a magnificent maple leaf. The ceremony reminded me of my childhood, when, before the morning exercises, we stood in rows in the school's large yard and, with our noses in the air, witnessed the raising of the flag with five stars, our little ears filled with the national anthem. I almost cried. I let out a sigh of relief, saying to myself: it's done, I made it, I will never again have to walk like a heroine on an arid path and under the indifferent sky; I'll be able to huddle up against my little lamp in my little nest, in peace. I was thirty years old that year. I had the impression of entering into a family where the parents are invisible, where the unknown brothers and sisters communicate in secret codes, where I was more fragile than ever, and had an overwhelming desire to please. I felt as if I were only three years old, there were still so many things to learn, to discover.

And in 1992, my first book was on the shelves in bookstores. It carries my name, but so many others lent a hand, among them Professor Yvon Rivard, the writer André Major and the editor Pierre Filion. I'm eternally grateful to them. I don't have to tell you what this event means to me. I think I am more myself when writing. I thank all those who accept and sometimes appreciate the real me. It wasn't a dialogue or a message, like you and many others thought. I don't have a message to deliver, any Chinese curios to display. I don't address myself to the outside world; I head for the inside. I want simply to get closer to my self, to explore as well as can be expected its evanescent and constantly renewed reality, to descend again and again into the depths of my being, into the depths of the land where boundaries aren't drawn, where even language is no longer important because you're approaching the essence of language. It happens that when the words flow well, I no longer know in which language they're coming to me. I'm transported by the mechanical and almost unconscious gesture of typing on the keyboard. And it's in this state that I hope finally to be able to meet the Other.

The publication of my first book marks such a meeting. A meeting with rare beings, of course: we can't hope that everyone will read our book, and in the same way. Above all, a book, like everything else, has its limits. But this meeting took place, I'm sure of it. It's easy for us to describe our solitude, because it's fundamental and constant. But how do we describe an instant of real happiness so short and intense? It resembles a spark, which seems to combine all our hopes within it, our past desires as well as our present momentum, and which therefore has the power to illuminate our entire life, past and future. Even though quickly extinguished, the tender memory of this spark will stay with us to warm our hearts in difficult times.

And difficult times—you've guessed it—are never lacking. Shortly after the happy events (the diploma, the book, my citizenship, etc.), something happened that made me fall from the cloud where I had taken refuge.

I was invited to a conference, this time as a Canadian writer, travelling for the first time on a Canadian passport. My Chinese passport was no longer valid. In the past, it had aroused a lot of attention, which I could understand, but this time I thought I had nothing to fear: I had one of the best passports in the world. I had forgotten the fact that my birthplace is indicated on my passport, that the sign of danger is written in my facial features.

Upon my return, during a stopover at the airport in Toronto, I was stopped, questioned and searched. That day, arriving in Toronto, I had rightly noticed a strange atmosphere at Customs. At the entrance booth, this extremely visible post, those charged with examining pockets and bags were uniquely "people of colour." And the search area, most of the time, was also reserved for "people of colour." I didn't see, in fact, one single person "without colour" on their way there. This situation is not entirely unfamiliar to me, but that day it was showing itself with striking clarity. A coincidence? The politically incorrect? The politically correct? In either case, I suddenly understood that there exists a solid, well-thought-out policy concerning immigrants, applied by an infallible machine, supported by an immense and ancient belief. And this policy can sometimes concern me— even me. The policy is always carried out with more rigour towards the apolitical or the politically weak, because it's less risky.

First I was asked what I could be doing "all alone" on this trip, which left me speechless. I became stupid under the shock, the way an animal freezes when faced with imminent danger. Then I was shown a secret door. I walked through it. I was in a dark room without windows. Prison could not be far away. I was shivering.

A police officer was waiting for me there, a very large man, and armed. His voice, hard as steel, prevented me from collapsing. "Put it here!" he said to me. He wanted me to lift my suitcase onto a kind of shelf, at a height that allowed him to touch it without bending his magisterial back too much. "Open it." And as I hesitated, he repeated, "Open it!" He didn't say please. It was therefore a familiar way of speaking. Not a familiar Quebec way of speaking, natural and simple; but a familiar French one, replete with provocation, insolence and contempt. All those who survived the Cultural Revolution would recognize this tone without fail. After having put his immense hand into my intimate belongings, in vain, the policeman contented himself with saying, "The door is over there." And he moved away, his back very straight and his head high.

I had time, alas, to notice that he was almost handsome. The muscles of his face seemed firm, full of conviction and assurance. I had hoped to find the marks of stupidity or monstrosity on his brow so that I could despise him. And that face without fault brought me that much more sorrow. As soon as I was liberated, I ran towards a mirror. Can you guess what I saw that day in the mirror? Stupidity and monstrosity. And I collapsed awhile on a bench, body and soul downcast.

My friends here will think me hypersensitive. They will tell me that this can happen to anyone. They will even give me examples. They don't understand. What I experienced was an authentic situation, where an authority and a subject, one armed and one disarmed, a man and a woman, faced each other without witness, in private, in a naked and unequivocal condition, and unveiled their inner selves without scruples or pretense; where each word and each gesture was charged with a profound tension, inexpressible but obvious to both. This kind of tension affects not only our reason; it first touches our senses. It's then we're sure of the thing. Only those who have known this kind of experience will understand what I mean.

That year, 1992, my new life was only three years old. I was desperately fragile. Sadly, childhood experiences are hard to erase, and the memory of this brutal encounter with a police officer at the airport will accompany me to the end.

Since then, I have been on the road again. Those who don't understand my condition would think that travelling is second nature to me. Sometimes I have to stop at borders and take out my Canadian passport, hesitating. Now I myself have doubts about this passport, which I'm no longer proud of. It doesn't seem to have the same value as the Canadian passports of others. So fear seizes me each time. And after each customs interrogation I need to sit down for a moment.

I've decided not to send you this letter, my dear friend, so that I'll no longer receive letters from you. I have written it in a language that you don't understand. (Here is one of the uses of knowing other languages.) Your letter touched me to the core, and it forced me, maybe a little too soon, to make a stop on my journey. I'm trying to see clearly what I could have had and don't have, what I could have given and have lost, in the past as well as the present, in your land as well as others. I don't like to show you such an outcome, as you would take it as proof of my failure. But I've neither failed nor succeeded. I don't speak in those terms. I've lived moments of joy, moments of desolation and years of solitude, that's all. If I had lived in another place, if I had stayed in Shanghai, the outcome would not be any better—probably worse.

It's important to me to be able to choose. I lived a long time in China, but I didn't choose it. I even had difficulties getting out, given the circumstances at the time. There's the nub of the problem. Now, at least, I live in a place of my own choosing. I even had the audacity to reproduce here. Sometimes I ask myself if a woman has the right to give birth when she hasn't even acquired solid ground, but I've never regretted making my children Canadians. They won't have an ancestral culture to vaunt and defend. And they won't be likely to go anywhere else permanently, because I believe they won't find another land that will be more favourable to them. Everything is relative. You say I'm not objective. Maybe it's true. You can't stay objective towards a place where your shell if not your soul has found its rest for years already. What vagabond doesn't dream of a roof, of a nest, of a grave? And as long as there are children, there's hope.

So, twelve years after the fall of my shell on this land, I am still walking towards it. I don't walk from one country to another, but from one place to another. The word "homeland" left my vocabulary the moment I left Shanghai. I don't have the desire to confuse my own fate with that of an entire nation. I wouldn't do it under any circumstance. I'm alone on my path. Patriotism of any kind troubles me, because I've suffered from it. Throughout my childhood I was isolated from the rest of the planet in the name of patriotism. I was searched like an enemy, a spy or a drug trafficker at the Toronto airport by a man who without doubt was patriotic to the bone. Spare me all this.

If a second birth is nothing but a play, I intend to perform it right to the end. Maybe I have two identities, as I've been told, but I have only one passport. It's an important fact. Concrete facts make us who we are. Roots are a luxury that beings like me can no longer dream about. We aren't able to keep them long in our pocket because it inevitably becomes worn with time, as our memory develops gaps. We become shifting trees whose roots cross over and around each other and lose themselves. We are transformed into a different species. Maybe it's what we always were, from the beginning, even before our voyage. And this new species, each day growing in number, rolls along a road that is, after all, solitary and ancient, without a precise destination, contented by approximations, because its own identity is constantly being formed.

But I need a reason to continue. I want to know where to go, precisely. I want to take daily steps. So I try to think that each day I'm approaching the land to which I will entrust my children, although I must still return to my own shell to fulfill my destiny. I think I've left my birthplace behind me and now I'm approaching the place where my journey ends. I'm glad to know approximately where I'll finish; it's not always evident amidst the dust of the road. I hope that wherever I'm put to rest, there won't be a flag or an inscription or a flower, but that nearby will be the sea, the sand, and grass without name.

———

Translated from the French by LEXique Ltd.

Moses Znaimer

———

D.P. WITH A FUTURE

IT IS DIFFICULT TO be sure whether what we think
of as our earliest memories are actual memories or
stories we were told when very young. Perhaps a pic-
ture of such a story forms in the imagination of the
child and, over time, takes on the detail and gravitas
of memory. As is the case with many Canadians
today, my earliest memories—whether they are in
fact stories told to me long ago or images that are
truly remembered—have to do with the passage from
a troubled place to a place of refuge.

We arrived in Canada in May 1948: Father,
Mother and me. That's all that was left. We were
post-war refugees from a displaced persons camp
outside a town called Kastle in Germany. Just getting
to that DP camp had been a saga for two frightened
Jewish kids, barely out of their teens, on the run from
the Nazis, each the survivor of a substantial family,
who had been thrown together by the fortunes of war
and had produced me in the middle of it all.

I now live and work in and out of Toronto, a city that has become to an exciting degree, a city of immigrants. When I step out of the ChumCityBuilding and walk along Queen Street West, I'm forever amazed at just how wonderfully diverse T.O. has become. But how many of those passersby, I wonder, are visited by memories of uncertain journeys, nervous anticipation, fear? People born and raised here can barely conceive of how many of their fellow citizens carry with them echoes of tragic events and places that seem all but impossible within our experience, here in the peaceable kingdom.

That's why I'm so proud of the strength my parents showed in completing the journey from that shattered old world to the promise of this new one. During that passage, how many times did Chaja and Aron swallow what must have been overwhelming dread, and press on? How many times did they look at their infant son and wonder what on earth the future could possibly hold for him? For them? I often think that one of the great strengths of this country is the simple courage that so many now-quiet, now-ordinary citizens showed in just getting here.

My father, Aron, was born in Kuldiga, Latvia, where his family was in the shoe business. He escaped on a borrowed bicycle minutes after hearing that the

Nazis were invading. It was June 22, 1941. My mother, Chaja, was Polish. She was born in Dubienka, and spent her teenage years in Lodz, where the family owned a stocking factory. Despite Chaja's "bourgeois" background, when the Russians occupied she got work in a munitions factory because of her education and was then evacuated to the Soviet Union as the Germans advanced. By the time she got together with Aron, she had acquired a Komsommol (Communist Youth) card, an indispensable entree to jobs and rations, and had done a stint in a *kolkhoz* (collective farm). She escaped with the help of an older man who fancied her. She then escaped from him too and, ever the confident one, approached Aron on a boat leaving Markstadt, when she heard him humming a familiar Yiddish tune.

Thus they began an epic journey of survival, moving constantly, east and south, marrying, and having their first child, Moses (*moi*), in Kulyab, Tajikistan, one of the Central Asian republics of the USSR. Aron had foresight. He always knew when it was time to leave, and at each stop they left behind young colleagues they would never see again. Chaja was shrewd and had a magical way of making friends—a quality that soon proved to be a lifesaver.

At that time, Aron was working in a granary.

He found himself accused of giving short measure. It turned out someone had tampered with the scales. It was wartime, and the penalty was death. He was arrested and interrogated by the dreaded NKVD (the Soviet secret police). Chaja, all of four foot ten and ninety pounds, bullied her way into a meeting with the prosecutor's wife. This connection, together with the gift of Aron's only valuable possession, a St. Moritz pen, secured his release and bought them enough time to finger the real culprit.

Because Aron had the foresight to use Chaja's surname, Epelzweig, instead of his own, the family was able to get out of the USSR when Polish nationals were repatriated after the war. Poland remained relatively porous and easy to get out of until the Iron Curtain was firmly brought down in 1947–48. So it was that a midnight rowboat ride across Berlin's Spree Canal brought us into the Western Zone.

After a stay in Hesse-Lichtenau, a DP camp in the American sector of occupied Germany, the three of us managed to emigrate to Canada. We steamed into Halifax harbour aboard a converted troopship, the SS *Marina Falcon*. From there we went by train to Montreal, where Aron had found two living relatives, our sponsors—"Auntie" Lina Goldberg and her son Gershon. And that's where, seven years later, in 1955, I was "naturalized" as a Canadian citizen. I've always liked that word *naturalized*, as if life before had been somehow unnatural, which, of course, it had been.

Two strong personal recollections emerge from the period before we got to Canada. One relates to food, the other to drink—not surprising, perhaps, given wartime shortages. Both, I have no doubt, are actual memories. In the first, I'm lying in my cot and Mother gives me a piece of bread. It's a warm crust that's been rubbed all over with garlic and baked with bits of the garlic pushed inside. Nothing could be simpler. It's so good, I start to cry.

In my second memory, some soldiers come by the camp mess and offer me a drink. It's cold and dark and sweet and effervescent—and I love it! When I get back to our barracks, I tell my parents about it, but they have no idea what it could be. In the following days and weeks I keep after them to get me that taste again. Was it dark beer? Was it kvass (a Russian drink made from black bread)? Was it strong, sweet iced tea? None of these! (Only when we were finally settled in Montreal and I tasted my first store-bought Coke did I realize what that treat had been. Even more wondrous was that something so scarce and unknown in that camp was, in my new world, available in every cooler, in every drugstore and corner store in town, for five cents.)

It's at this point—our arrival at the DP camp in the American Zone of occupied Germany—that my memories start to accumulate into something certain. This is where I begin to have my own stories. One of the most vivid of these has to do with some munitions that a couple of playmates and I found in a stream near the camp.

Towards the end of the war, piles of ammo, big machine-gun bullets and larger shells, were dumped in that stream, by a retreating army, I imagine. This day, we are amusing ourselves by fishing them out and trying to set them off. An adult comes upon us just as I raise a howitzer-type cartridge in my hand, poised to smash its base on a rock. He lets out a wild holler and starts to run towards me, gesticulating wildly. I drop it and take off. He follows. He chases me into a nearby abandoned building. (In retrospect, I'm sure he was only concerned for our well-being, but at the time his determination frightened me.) I get away by jumping out of the second floor of that bombed-out building. It's quite a leap, and I wake up the next day with a serious hernia as a result.

This is bad news. Our longed-for emigration to Canada depends on passing our medicals. So, prior to mine, I am literally tied down to keep me from jumping about, and on board ship, and later on shore, the hernia is suppressed with a truss.

Remember, I was born in the early 1940s in wartime Tajikistan—not the most developed place in the world even today—where, needless to say, health conditions were not what they might have been. Infant mortality was murderously high. Modern Western medicines, vaccines, and even simple preventatives like clean water and sterilized instruments were not readily available. As a result, unprotected from some of the world's most dangerous diseases, I immediately, in the first hours and days of my life, contracted—and, in a curious way, was thus inoculated against—malaria, hepatitis, TB and who knows what else.

I survived, obviously, and in fact grew up quite robust, thereby demonstrating the truth of the old adage that what doesn't kill you makes you stronger. The only problem was that the antibodies I had acquired were still present in my system, and my anxious parents feared that I would test positive for TB and the rest. Quite rightly, they suspected that the Canadian authorities would not be very interested in the fine distinction between my unusual condition and that of a carrier of some extremely dangerous diseases.

As a result, Aron and Chaja hatched a scheme, as ingenious as it was brazen, to get me past the famous TB patch test, which I would surely fail. They simply substituted another child—a boy about my age, the son of DP camp friends and neighbours—and presented him to the authorities in my place. He passed with flying colours, and it was his certificate that finally got us on board the *Marina Falcon*. Apparently, he and his family left for what would soon become Israel around the same time that we sailed for Canada.

While the hernia caper and the TB switcheroo make for great stories today, both ruses troubled my parents, in particular my mother. It's probably a common fear among would-be emigrants, especially refugees, that at some stage in their difficult and dangerous escape, one overzealous official, or a small bureaucratic detail, will block their passage and make them return to what they are so desperately fleeing. My mother was never entirely free of this nightmare, and even in the safety of Montreal, years after our escape, she lived in apprehension of being caught. This insecurity isn't something you can shake, forget or leave behind; it infiltrates dreams, and the habit of constant worry and vigilance never goes away. My mom always half expected to hear the proverbial knock on the door. She was haunted by the worry that someone, somewhere, would notice a discrepancy, would compare two forms and say, "Hey wait a minute . . ."

The substitute boy's name was Yosel. That's all I know: not a family name, not a nickname, not a single distinguishing feature. It's a measure of just how spooked my parents were about the entire episode that they never told me anything more. I guess they thought the less said the better, lest something inadvertently slip out of a child's mouth at the wrong time, in the wrong place.

In fact, I might have gone to Israel too, like Yosel, but for the Jewish politics of the day. In his youth, my father had been a passionate member of a Jewish self-defence organization whose founder also led a centre-right party in the then nascent Zionist movement. The big point of dispute between the right and the dominant left wing of that movement was whether or not Jews should fight. The majority argued that militarism was not in the tradition. My dad and the party he belonged to felt that the precarious, too often persecuted condition of Jews around the world could only be alleviated if Jews too had a territory to call their own and a strong army to protect them.

With the end of World War II and the full realization of the extent and horror of the Holocaust, this argument was joined with particular ferocity. Where were the Jewish survivors to go? Who would take them in? How would they get there? Many dreamt of the peace and economic prospects of the New World, but Zionists believed that Jewish life could only become "normal" in the Promised Land. As Palestine was then under a British mandate, and as the British responded to Arab resistance to increased Jewish immigration by allowing in only a legal trickle, illegal immigration boats were organized to run the blockade. Some boatloads made it ashore. Many didn't, and Jewish refugees once again found themselves behind barbed wire, this time in British detention camps on Cyprus. These boats were under the control of the Zionist left, who, moreover, controlled much of the civic machinery of what would eventually become the State of Israel. But they reserved those desperately scarce, desperately wanted places for their own partisans. So, no room for Dad. No room for us.

Instead, we went sailing, legally, into the eerie calm of Canada—a country without conscription—while Yosel and his family sailed off into the Israeli War of Independence, followed by the Six Day War, which was followed by the Yom Kippur War, which was followed by the Iraqi Scuds of Desert Storm, all accompanied by the never-ending wear and tear of constant terrorism. I wonder if Yosel ever made it. I wonder if that boy who, for a few crucial hours, pretended to be me is still alive, and if so, where?

I also wonder what would have happened if the Znaimers had never got out of the Soviet Union in the first place. I shudder to think how I, a free-enterprising, freethinking nonconformist might have fared amid the anti-Semitic paranoia of Stalinist Russia, with its ubiquitous secret police; or in the stultifying collectivism of the period that followed; or during the collapse of the Soviet Union itself. There but for the grace of God . . .

Of our two-week passage to Canada on that converted troop carrier, I remember a stormy Atlantic, my parents deathly seasick down below and me on my own, hanging out with the sailors, including the very first black man I'd ever seen. I remember the vast sheds where we new arrivals were slowly processed; then another long train trip; and finally, Montreal.

Immediately, I was sent to a hospital for my hernia. Cut off from the Yiddish, German, Russian, Polish, Latvian, Hebrew and God knows what else that flew around my milieu, I came out, two weeks later, with a functional command of English and quite a few colourful words of French.

Aron's first job in Canada was as a pants and blouse presser, and Chaja began work in a bakery. We settled into a third-floor walk-up on St-Urbain Street. Libby and Sam, my sister and brother, were born. Chaja continued to work. Aron was reunited with his sister Becky, who had managed to escape to Northern Rhodesia. Of that generation she was the only surviving sibling on either side.

Eventually, Aron was able to open a small shoe store, but his heart wasn't in business. Every spare moment, his head was in a book; he could savour a newspaper all day. Although Saturday was the busiest day of the retail week, he would be happiest if there were few customers so that he could sit in the back listening to *Live at the Metropolitan Opera*.

Chaja became a waitress, or at least that was her title. She essentially ran a successful steak house for a Damon Runyon character whose clientele included Jimmy the Book and Obie the Butcher. In addition to serving, she did the ordering and bookkeeping, and played mother confessor to a staff worthy of a soap opera. She was always grateful to be working and never dreamed she was being exploited, though we were convinced she was. Chaja never got over the loss of her entire family. It was a black hole she didn't let us into, and we barely know the names of all the Epelzweigs. However, she built a new extended family, the "Kollezshankes," a group of immigrant women who were like sisters to her until the day she died.

Our parents lived for their children, working endless hours at jobs they did not love. They gave us a great education, a sense of independence, and a love of learning and Jewish culture. Though they were earning breadcrumbs—she as a waitress, he as a presser and shoe salesman—still they found a way to send me to the United Talmud Torah. UTT was a "parochial" or private school, and cost precious extra money we didn't have. In the Quebec education system, all schools were held to be denominational, with the world crudely divided into Catholic and Protestant school boards. If you weren't Catholic and couldn't afford or didn't care to go to a Jewish school, you could go to a public one, called Protestant even if 99 percent of the student body were Jewish. That was the case at the famous Baron Byng High School that Mordecai Richler attended, which was around the corner from our own Herziliah, the high school extension of UTT. I stayed in the parochial system all the way through matriculation, until I started at McGill.

Looking back on it now, I see I was lucky to have that experience. The education was rigorous: half a day in Hebrew, for religious and cultural studies; half a day in English, pursuing an enriched form of the standard curriculum. On Saturdays we held our own "junior congregation" in the school gym. I led the services as cantor and was pretty good at it. In fact, I developed a bit of a following, mostly Orthodox girls who would come every week to catch my solos. It was my first taste of performing, of being in the spotlight, and of what we would today call groupies.

The overflow of American McCarthyism into the Canada of the day threw a few more elements of a non-traditional upbringing my way—most notably in the person of the great Canadian poet Irving Layton. Temporarily denied access to the universities, where he properly belonged, and unable to make a living solely from his writing, he taught English literature and history and grammar at Herziliah. He was an enormous influence on me, and indeed on many of the students. He had an extremely powerful personality—one that I was actually wary of, because I didn't want simply to ape him, as several of my classmates did. Layton was the centre of a kind of literary cult, and I'm not much of a follower. But I was happy to be inspired by him—inspired to believe that words, ideas, art and education matter; inspired to believe that thinkers, writers and doers matter. Layton demanded that we read a wide range of material. He interrogated us, debated with us, performed for us. He was also my first real connection to the world of media, which would later become my life. I remember him returning to class in triumph after having been "all the way" to Toronto, mixing it up with the celebrated theatre critic Nathan Cohen on the nationally televised CBC program *Fighting Words*.

Another part of my education derived from outside school. In fact, my extracurricular activities were probably as formative as my long days and years in class. I worked as a delivery boy, as a tutor, as a pin boy in a bowling alley. I worked as a waiter in a country club set up by wealthy Jews who'd been turned away from establishment WASP clubs. Most Sundays I sang at weddings—a dollar and a half if in the choir, three bucks if I did the solo, plus all the hors d'oeuvres I could eat. I got to wear a white silk caftan and a high domed cap, but even so grandly attired, and especially because my rendition of that great Mario Lanza hit "Because" invariably stole the show, I knew I was being exploited by what Layton called the "Booboisie." So I took full advantage of the privileges of the hors d'oeuvres table, once managing to eat sixty cocktail hot dogs between two engagements. Sweet revenge! Terrible tummy ache!

In the middle and late 1950s, Montreal was justifiably called the Paris of North America. Despite its apparently oppressive Catholicism, it was open and full of excitement, sophistication, exoticism, grit, sleaze. The city had theatre and jazz and a joie de vivre that distinguished it from the pinched cultural wasteland that was Toronto. One of my jobs landed me pretty much at the centre of Montreal nightlife. Friday and Saturday nights, I worked as a busboy at one of the city's most notorious nightclubs, the Chez Paris, on Stanley Street. It had pretty much everything: strippers, homosexuals, gamblers, the soap opera that was the kitchen staff, the rich rounders as well as the poseurs, and the endlessly entertaining night owls who frequented such an establishment. I loved it, and being underage and quite cute, I made out like a bandito.

When my school found out I was working there, I was called into the principal's office and informed that a worthy member of the community had agreed to cover my school fees in order that I would not have to spend any more time at so disreputable an address. I was aghast and refused on the spot, and was promptly expelled for three days to contemplate my ingratitude. But I hung on to my gig until a year or two later, when the club was smashed up in a gang war.

Thus, education was for me an adventure rather than a hardship, whereas for my parents it was a reward for long years of struggle. After seven years of night school, Aron earned a BA in Jewish Studies from Concordia University. He was seventy-two. It was his proudest achievement. After retiring, Chaja studied for two years and received a diploma in Gerontology from Collège Marie-Victorin. As usual, she developed close friendships with people from different backgrounds, including an Anglican priest who became a regular at our Passover Seders.

Aron and Chaja were devoted to each other. While caring for Aron in his final illness, Chaja ignored her own health. Aron died in February 1992, Chaja in November 1993. They did not live to see what would have been their greatest joy—the birth of their grandchildren, to my brother, Sam, and his partner, Lesley Stalker. Leith Aron was born three weeks after Chaja passed away. His sister, little Chaya, arrived in May 1997.

For a child, being "stateless" and on the run is not all bad. You see the world, you pick up languages, you hear different styles of music and eat a variety of foods. You begin to understand the richness of the world and the joys to be had from being open to all kinds of people and cultures. Even before starting grade school, I'd already lived through aspects of a world war and taken a hazardous trip that crossed many borders. These experiences left me a cocky little kid with a strong sense of self.

It was a different story for my parents. For all their remarkable qualities, the capacity for happiness had been irretrievably killed in them. A gloom settled over everything. We were survivors, and one aspect of being a survivor is learning to keep your head down. I was not encouraged to go out and conquer the world. On the contrary, I was brought up to be grateful that we weren't being killed in the streets or sent to the ovens. Above all, I was taught not to make trouble. Though I was a dutiful son and respected my parents enormously, it was a lesson I never learned . . .

All immigrants feel that they are the last ones. I know I did. They think they're on the bottom of the totem pole that leads to success and respect in Canadian life, and that everyone else is ahead of them in power and privilege. Of course, it's not true. The inflow is perpetual, and yesterday's refugees are tomorrow's establishment, or at least their kids are.

Still, I identify with all newcomers and have my fingers crossed for every one of them. I've lived their drama of struggling with a new language, of absorbing a new culture while trying to hang on to old traditions. But hard work and zeal for self-improvement actually do bring results in this blessed part of the world. Our little remnant of a family found in Canada a haven of tolerance in a land of opportunity. I'm sure they will too.

―――

Dany **Laferrière**

—

ONE-WAY TICKET

1. The car rolled quickly along, weaving across the
    many cracks full of green water. The city looked
    newly bombed. We were coming back from a night-
    club in the southern suburb of Port-au-Prince.
    Around two o'clock in the morning. My city at
    night. Almost nobody on the barely lit streets. Here
    and there, large, thin dogs watched us pass with an
    almost scornful indifference. Five in the car: two
    women (a Russian and a Yugoslavian) and three
    Haitian men. I was dozing, in the back, jammed
    between the two young women. They were jour-
    nalists, here to secretly make a documentary about
    Haiti. I had been their guide for the past week, an
    extremely dangerous situation at the beginning of
    that year—1976. The international press was begin-
    ning to demand explanations from Duvalier junior.
    The authorities were getting restless.

    The driver, a young doctor, wanted us to
    visit the general hospital in Port-au-Prince. The

journalists woke up right away. They filmed
everything. I was appalled to see the pitiful condition of the state hospital. I knew the place well:
I went there often to count the dead. At the time,
I was working for a weekly political and cultural
newspaper (*Le Petit Samedi Soir*) that questioned
the propaganda of the governing elite, who continued to claim things had changed for the better
in Haiti, that Duvalier junior (Baby Doc) was
different from his father (Papa Doc). I knew the
hospital by day, but at night it was something
else: the epicentre of suffering. All those people
howling in pain, without a nurse to bring them
even a Tylenol. Live pain. Twisted faces. You got
the impression that these patients, almost participating in the government propaganda by day,
finally let themselves go at night. I had the feeling (stimulated by the wan light) that I was
descending into Dante's infernal circles. The little spotlight above the camera searched tirelessly
for a new case more dramatic than the last.
Abruptly, the country presented itself naked
before me.

I was twenty-three years old, and I didn't yet
know that I would have to leave Haiti a few days
later under truly dramatic circumstances. Indeed

I learned, some time later, that my best friend
(also a journalist at *Le Petit Samedi Soir*) had been
assassinated by Baby Doc's Tontons Macoutes
not too far from the place where I had just been
dancing. Dancing on the volcano. Learning that I
was next on the death squad's blacklist, my mother arranged for me to leave the country hastily.

2. I disembarked in Montreal one '76 summer morning, in the midst of Olympic euphoria. The
immigration officers were trying to spot any ter-
rorist arrivals in the crowd. Some African countries had decided to boycott the Montreal games
because of the participation of South Africa. And
even in the airplane itself the rumour circulated
that because of the African boycott, blacks
weren't being warmly welcomed in Montreal.

People have no idea of the number of
rumours that circulate in an airplane coming from
the Third World. It's a wonder how false tourists,
coming from the poorest countries on the planet,
can, without even leaving the plane or receiving
any information besides that concerning the
weather, know in such detail the frame of mind of
the Canadian immigration officers. Someone on
the plane remarked that these expulsion measures

didn't concern us for the simple reason that, even if we were black like them, we were not Africans but Haitians. It must be made known to the Canadian authorities before we were driven away because of our colour. In this case it would be racism, a woman said. Someone added that you could possibly understand the rather brutal attitude of the Canadian officers towards the Africans who boycotted the games (even if they had a good reason to do it), but extending this to the Haitians, who were participating with a strong delegation of three athletes accompanied by twelve officials, could be nothing but pure racism. Is it necessary to explain that Haiti isn't Africa? All blacks are not Negroes. The Haitians, who won their independence from Napoleonic France by blood and by sword, on that first of January, 1804, continue to refuse to be confused with those Africans who didn't gain their independence until recently, in the 1960s. Well, it's like that in Haiti: patriotism is never far away. And a spark can light the powder keg. It was for good reason that a Haitian friend, describing the difference between Quebec and Haiti, said later that if in Quebec blood smells like eau de cologne, in Haiti it's the eau de cologne that smells like blood.

I think we were almost ready to land when a man behind me suggested that in a case like this (the boycott of the Olympic Games because of the presence of South Africa), we should align ourselves with our African brothers. All the Haitians on the plane applauded and promised to refuse the Canadian entry visa to protest the participation of South Africa in the Montreal games. Naturally, everyone knew it would happen differently in reality.

3. I had a strangely easy time with the immigration officer. The usual questions were asked. I was well prepared. A friend who had already lived in Canada had explained the matter to me: the only thing the immigration officers hate is when you don't respond directly to their questions. In Haiti, it's straight-out impolite simply to answer a question. It's imperative to make a little digression; otherwise the speaker receives his answer like a slap in the face. When I was asked my name, while the officer held my passport in his hand, with my name spelled out in full, I didn't think, like my predecessor, that the immigration officer didn't know how to read, or even that he thought I was an idiot. I simply told myself that

Canadians (at that time in Haiti, Quebec didn't exist; we knew only Canada, which to us was a totally French country) are different from Haitians. That's another good reason to travel.

The immigration officer quickly understood that I was ready to co-operate. To him, a man from the Third World who directly answers questions that appear common (name and address, for example), without attempting any supplementary explanation, well, this man has already made half the journey towards the dreamed-of integration in the welcoming country. The idea is to quickly make good little Canadians out of these immigrants, to have them swallow the habits and customs of the country as fast as possible. The officer smiled at me as he returned my passport.

4. Here I am already at the airport customs. There is an enormous woman right in front of me, in a heated discussion with the customs officer.

The customs officer: Have you declared these mangoes, madame?

The large woman: Where are the mangoes? These aren't mangoes!

The customs officer: But, madame, I see mangoes right here . . .

The large woman: These aren't mangoes . . . I can tell you this because I'm the one who planted the mango tree. And it was this morning, just before running to the airport, that I went to pick these mangoes myself.

The customs officer: I understand all that, madame, but these mangoes—

The large woman: Why are you calling them mangoes? I just explained to you that they aren't mangoes in the sense you mean . . .

The customs officer makes a weary gesture with his hand to say he's throwing in the towel. And the large woman, with a magnificent smile, pushes her cart full of heavy suitcases towards the exit.

5. She won, but how far will Canada accept this strange way of seeing life? Mangoes that are not to be called mangoes? Of course there's the other debate, about the individual's place in society. In the south (or the Third World), the human being is even more important than the laws (although the Tontons Macoutes often mistake us for wild ducks). It's for this reason that there's a difficulty there in obeying the Constitution. Each person expects to be treated on a personal level, and what he has to say in his defence always seems more

precious to him than any rule. In the north, institutions exist precisely to prevent the citizen from believing he can be a singular entity. We're all equal here; only collective harmony prevails. In Haiti, anarchy reigns. And despite the terrible dictatorship that crushes them, people firmly believe that their social organization is preferable to that found in Western countries. In Haiti, everything revolves around the individual, in a negative way (dictatorship) as well as a positive way (one who maintains that a mango is not always a mango would easily be believed). Why? Well, because at the end of the day a human being is more important to us than a mango.

This way of seeing the world can sometimes put you into a certain state of confusion. I knew early on that I would have to become a maroon, at least intellectually, if I didn't want to lose my mind. In my case it meant pretending to accept a culture while trying by every means to blow it up. But you can't hold this position for long. Flight is all that remains.

6. Marooning is an old technique that goes back to colonial times. The maroon is the slave who flees the plantation to find his free brothers in the

mountains. Of course, the maroon Negro is always on the alert, constantly expecting to see his masters arrive with the dogs. This is a man who eats quickly, sleeps little, invents a number of codes to communicate with the other maroons, and often changes locations to protect himself.

Despite independence, the maroons haven't changed their ways. They're recognizable because they don't have confidence in anyone, they keep everything secret (name, address, date of birth, phone number) and they never share their true thoughts. Be careful: these are not paranoiacs— they are maroons. The paranoiac, in a feverish way, believes he is surrounded by enemies, while the maroon sets himself up, very serenely, in a kind of long-term underground. His deepest self remains impenetrable. From his point of view the notion of cultural integration seems to be one of the most sinister Judaeo-Christian jokes.

7. Here I am in the city. In Montreal. People are celebrating. The Olympic Games represent the most important event (both social and sporting) since the Universal Exposition in 1967. I'm very happy to come across a city in full effervescence. The obvious joy that I see on the faces of the

Montrealers is a nice change from the Haitian drama. It's the middle of summer. The girls are wearing such short skirts, it puts me on edge. Young people are kissing each other on the mouth in the streets. It's so new. To tell the truth, everything is new for me. And even today, twenty-five years later, I'm still stunned by this change. I had just left a country so closed sexually, so harsh politically, so terrible socially (hunger, health, education), to come so abruptly to the Montreal of 1976.

The first thing that impressed me was the absence of Tontons Macoutes, those hoodlums armed by the state. I will always remember the first time I witnessed an altercation between a policeman and a young hippie. The aggressive hippie was almost insulting (in fact he was only defending his rights), while the policeman kept his cool. Finally, the policeman left without having been able to make the young man leave the park bench where he was lying. I didn't understand this country where a young hoodlum (in Haiti, anyone dressed this way could be nothing but a hoodlum) could thwart the police. At the end, the smiling hippie made a sign that could have been Churchill's V for victory or the peace sign. Was it to let me know that he had defeated the dragon or to welcome me in a brotherly way to his territory?

8. Scarcely two weeks later, I was walking calmly down a dark little street when a car stopped abruptly behind me. When someone started shouting at me quite harshly, I turned around to see two guns pointed my way. In an instant, I was spread out on the hood of a police car, legs apart. Standard procedure. My situation was complicated by the fact that I didn't understand what they were saying. They spoke with a thick *joual* accent. Well, I said to myself, the only way to act in front of a policeman, no matter where in the world, is to be silent and keep your head down. Here's the first big lesson that I learned instinctively in North America.

One of the policemen got into the car while the other continued to keep me in firing range. The first came back out a moment later and told me I could leave. He said it in a tone that was still aggressive, as though he were truly devastated to let a criminal go free. I walked a little before turning around to face them. I know it was reckless on my part, but I couldn't let it end this way.

"Why did you call me over?" I asked in a polite tone.

The two policemen gave me a surprised look. As I wasn't moving, one of them said, "We're looking for a black man."

And the other added, "Don't play cute with us!"

I didn't exactly understand the expression, but I knew he wanted to make me understand that I had, by asking the question, crossed a boundary.

I went over the two events with a fine-tooth comb for a good day in order to understand, beyond racism, what the difference was between them. With the young hippie, it happened during the day and in a busy public park. Maybe the policemen who work by day in the Latin district are different from those who operate at night in the dark alleys. Or if they're the same, they have different mandates. So the same hippie, at night, in a dark alley, with two policemen searching for a criminal, would have behaved differently than he did in the park (he wouldn't have been so sure of his rights). Another point caught my attention: the accent. I hadn't quite understood what the policemen were saying. Of course, I had adopted the universally accepted behaviour in front of a policeman: silence. But it wouldn't be sufficient in future. I would have to plunge into Quebec culture right away, not only to understand what

was said around me, but also to be able to quickly decipher the gestures, the signs, everything left
unsaid in this new culture. Otherwise, I was a
man in danger.

9. I get into a taxi downtown.
    "I'm French," says the driver. "I've been liv-
ing here for forty years now."
    "Do you like it?" I ask shyly.
    "If I didn't like it, old man . . . I like the win-
ters, people are very friendly, but from a cultural
point of view, it's the desert."
    "I arrived barely a few weeks ago . . ."
    "Your French is good. I don't understand how
people can massacre such a beautiful language like
they do here. I've been in this country forty years
now and I'm still not used to their accent. They
have an atrocious accent, don't you think?"
    I don't dare tell him that, as I see it, all accents
are of equal merit. Let's just say I find it scan-
dalous that, after forty years in a country, someone can still have such prejudices. For the
moment, the people here are still "them" to me,
but I'm anxious for "them" to become "us."
Because if I'm here, it's really my choice and not
theirs. So it's up to me to adapt.

"Montreal has changed a lot, I believe, since your arrival . . ."

"A lot. When I first arrived here, in '36, there was nothing. Now there's the metro, the stadium—a very nice stadium—Expo 67, it was quite an expo . . . It must be said that everything started with the Expo."

"I see it's a big city today."

He shakes his head. "Not yet. I'm used to finding all kinds of things at any time in a big city, and we're not there yet in Montreal . . . New York is a big city . . ."

"Paris too," I say.

"Ah, Paris," he says. "Paris is . . . Paris. But I like the people here. They're not pretentious like they are in Paris. I go back to France less and less often. I don't like the life back there any more."

"Here, it's only the accent that bothers you, if I understand correctly . . ."

A pause. He seems to think about it.

"I'm ashamed to say it, but I miss the real bread too. Especially when I've finished working around five in the morning, if I could find some good bread, I would never think about France again."

"Some real bread, an interesting cheese and a good bottle of wine . . ."

"I don't ask for all that—only some bread."

"One day it'll happen . . ."

"I don't despair."

10. I arrive at the home of a friend I knew in Haiti. He lives in a small room on Saint-Hubert Street, just behind the Terminus Voyageur. He is cooking. I look at him a moment. It is the first time I have seen a Haitian man cooking. He's been in Montreal for eleven years.

"Who taught you how to cook?"

"You'll never guess," he answers. "A Quebecker. She had married a Haitian and her mother-in-law had taught her to cook Haitian food."

"It's not like in the United States, here. The Quebeckers, I see, marry Haitians easily."

"They don't think we're black. Here, we're Haitians instead. Actually, Quebeckers call themselves the White Negroes of North America."

"Yeah? You mean they're not racist?"

"Not at all. One of the reasons I left Haiti is the racism. I didn't understand such violent racism between people of the same race. Each spits on the one who's more black than him."

"It's the colonial heritage."

"When someone sinks a knife into my back, I don't want to know if it's because of his unhappy childhood."

"Meanwhile, it was a white Quebec woman who taught you how to cook Haitian food."

"Exactly. They love Haitian cooking. And since they've been eating Haitian dishes, they're starting to get Negro bottoms. And, old man, that's all they were missing."

"What are you talking about?"

"When I arrived here, the girls were magnificent—face, hair, legs, all perfect. But no bottoms. From behind, they looked like Chinese taxi drivers. Then they started to eat yams, plantains, pork, sweet potatoes and lots of rice. So, as the years passed, they started to get bottoms. Real white Negro women."

"And the Haitian women weren't happy?"

"They went into a terrible rage, but the harm was already done."

"I don't understand why you prefer a white Negro woman, as you say, to the real Negro."

"The Haitian woman, before this competition, had an unbelievable arrogance. You had to marry her to be able to kiss her, and when you married her, you had the added responsibility of a large and demanding family overnight. But since the Quebec women have joined the game, they had to start taking it easy. There's nothing like a little competition to ease the game."

"I'm hungry."

"We'll eat in a minute."

11. I discovered the well-to-do suburbs of Montreal with Paul, a friend with whom I did Canada World Youth. His parents were friendly. The father was a fierce Péquiste. The mother was interested in nothing but her family. It was in this house that I learned about politics in Quebec. I thought people here didn't discuss politics; that the head of state was a good father, Catholic, who ran his country like his family. I quickly learned that it's much more complex than it appears. Don't trust the innocent face, the country fragrance or that kind of farmers' honesty (at first I thought Quebeckers didn't know how to lie) that floats in the air.

Upon arrival you get the impression that this is a country without a past. But no, they too had a strong man who dominated their conscience (for me it was Duvalier senior; for them it was Duplessis). Duvalier reigned in Haiti with the help of voodoo, by playing on the people's ancestral fear; Duplessis counted on the help of the Catholic Church. Duvalier often relied on nationalism to stay in power; Duplessis as well. Fortunately, Duplessis didn't have any Tontons Macoutes. The difference lies in the methods used by each of the two peoples to get through this era of great darkness. Haitians, obsessed with history, wanted to deal with the problem only on the political front. Quebeckers carried out a Quiet Revolution based on education and the secularization of the public authorities—and on culture too. They ended up opening the windows wide. Fresh air rushed into the house. Haitians are still wading through the mud of dictatorship.

12. This morning, I am sitting in front of Paul's father at the breakfast table. Paul is sleeping off last night's drinks.

"But really! Really! I never would have believed this: Claude Ryan asking us to vote for the Parti Québécois in his editorial in *Le Devoir*."

Le Devoir is Quebec's big intellectual daily newspaper. Someone has recently explained to me that *Le Devoir* is to Quebec what *Le Monde* is to France. Paul's father passes me the newspaper.

A long, copious editorial full of nuances and reservations, saying he is opposed to the raison d'être of the party for which he is asking people to vote (in the pure Jesuit tradition). In Haiti, you think of nothing but physically eliminating your political adversary. Here, you're asked to vote for him if it seems reasonable: *reason*. In Haiti, a political adversary is an enemy: *passion*. Good Lord! I'm not going to fall for Senghor's formula which asserts that "Reason is Greek, and emotion, black."

"What's the importance of an editorial like this?" I ask.

"Huge. When your worst enemy comes around to your side, there's no better propaganda."

"And what will happen when the Parti Québécois comes into power?"

"They'll finally ask the question. They'll ask Quebeckers if they want to live in an independent country or stay a province."

"Well, in Haiti we had a national war to gain our independence. I never thought a country could become independent simply by asking its citizens: do you want to be independent?"

He looks at me worriedly. I have just spoiled the pleasure the editorial in *Le Devoir* provided him. What a misunderstanding! I am in total admiration of the founding work done by the Quebec people. I prefer the calm morning to the bloody twilight.

13. A Haitian woman, about forty-five years old. Chickens on sale in a local supermarket. Very good price. Only two chickens per customer. She had taken five, and it seemed impossible to make her understand the rules of the game. The manager of the supermarket had called the police.

"Madame," said the policeman calmly, "you can't take more than two chickens."

"Really, sir, I'm not taking the chickens, I'm buying them."

"Fine. You can't *buy* more than two chickens."

"I'm not stealing, I'm paying with my own money, and I don't know why a policeman should get involved. We're a democracy here."

Note that people who've lived under a dictatorship are always very sensitive to the idea of democracy, especially when it's in their interest.

"If you aren't happy, madame, you can return to your country."

And the retort came instantly. "At least I have a country."

The policeman lightly stroked his cheek. I felt he was within an inch of exploding. The problem is, this woman has only one thing in life, but it's the one thing that so many Quebeckers would love to have: an independent country.

14. I spent Friday night with Paul's friends. We went to a small island with a few cases of Molson beer, some marijuana and a little music. Guys and girls. It took me some time to understand that for the guys, the point of the night wasn't to sleep with the girls. We mostly talked about Surrealists. Poets: Breton, Éluard. Painters: especially Dali. I didn't understand. The father completely obsessed with the coming election; the son saturated with Surrealism. Where's the link? I tried to smoke a bit. It was no use. It did nothing for me. I'm told that the first time, it doesn't happen right away; you have to wait. I waited. Nothing.

So I started to look at the girls and to listen much less attentively to the debate about the difference between Dali and Picasso. I quickly spotted a tall, thin girl who also seemed not to care about Dali. I went to sit beside her. She was sweet and kind. I took her hand, like that. I pretended to read her heart line. At a given moment she bent over to kiss me. My whole body was trembling. It was slightly chilly, mid-November. We kissed for a long time. My first Quebec kiss. I liked her smell. We had made a fire, and her hair smelled of smoke. And also that smell that I couldn't determine. The smell of the other. I myself must also have a particular smell. The accent or the smell—nobody can escape it. No perfume can mask your intimate smell. She started to caress me. I felt a bit embarrassed in front of the others, who were watching us.

"Your brother looks angry," I said to her.

"That's not my brother, it's my boyfriend."

"You mean your lover."

"If you want," she said, while kissing me as though she were going to devour my mouth.

I opened my eyes to find the guy still looking at me.

"What's wrong?"

"I can't with this guy in front of me."

"OK," she said, guiding me to the other side of the island.

I had the impression I was her prey, an unknown sensation for a young man in the Caribbean, except with a rich older woman. I learned so many things in just one night. And from the same girl.

15. I find the group again in Paul's cellar. They are listening to music. Heavy metal. It's the tradition here: the more the parents' music seems policed, the more the children's music has to seem barbaric. They're still passing around the marijuana, asking themselves if one day they might exhibit their paintings.

"Why don't you show them here?" I ask.

"Where?" Paul asks me.

"Here, in the sitting room. There's lots of space."

"But we can't!"

"Why?"

"It's not a gallery."

"Big difference! You hang the paintings on the wall. People come to see them. You offer refreshments. And if someone wants to buy one, you give him a price."

Silence. Suddenly, a cry from Paul: "This guy is brilliant!"

Despite the marijuana, the heavy metal music and the fact that young Quebeckers can spend the night with anyone, I get the impression that, on a deeper level, young Haitians are freer. Let's say definitely more responsible. When poverty is mixed with dictatorship, it gives people a more precocious sense of responsibility.

They become interested in me.

"Are there painters where you come from?"

"We do nothing but that. In Haiti, painting is a popular art. All my neighbours paint to earn a living. Our main goal isn't to have social status as a painter, but to live from this work."

"And music?"

"It's only for dancing. We never sit like you're doing to listen to music. Music goes with the body. There's a direct link."

"What kind of dancing?" asks my friend from last night, who seems to be a dancer herself. It's true she has a body made for ballet.

"You cling to the girl and try to become one with her. Dancers can kiss, too. In fact, they make love standing up, to the music. It's called vertical fucking."

"I could never do that," she says. "For me they're two such absorbing things. When I listen to music, it's as though I were living in a universe of pure sound. When I dance, it's the same thing but with colours."

"Three things," her boyfriend says calmly. "Johanne, you're forgetting love."

"That must be something, to dance while

making love," says another girl, Sylvie, giving me a languorous look.

"We do this in Haiti only because there's a lack of space. Port-au-Prince is an overpopulated city. It's in the crowd of dancers that you generally manage to find a certain intimacy."

"That's something I'd like to try," says Sylvie.

What I immediately understood when I arrived here is that the Quebec woman is more open than the man, more apt to plunge into a new society. The man refuses to leave his familiar place, as though he were constantly in danger, from a cultural point of view, while the woman seems more audacious. She's capable of penetrating into the young immigrant's bedroom. She wants to know everything: what he eats, his music, his dance and also his way of making love. Integration is a fundamentally masculine idea. It seems to me it's very close to sexual penetration. The immigrant must let himself be penetrated by the welcoming country's culture before being accepted into the tribe, while the female body is made for welcoming—to be penetrated. The woman is therefore North America's soft belly, and our only chance to keep a part of our past alive.

16. In a Haitian taxi. Montreal. November 16, 1976 (the day after the victory of the Parti Québécois).

The driver turns towards me. "You're Haitian?"

"Yes," I say.

"You watched the election yesterday?"

"Magnificent! The Parti Québécois is finally in power."

"How long have you been here?" he asks in a fairly brutal tone.

"Five months."

"OK, I'm going to tell you something. This country belongs to the Haitians. We're everywhere. In the schools, in the hospitals (and not only as patients), in the factories, everywhere. With the taxi, we control the road, day and night. We know exactly what's happening in politics before everyone else. Last week, I drove Premier Bourassa in my taxi twice. And we talked at length. Mr. Bourassa understood that the importance of Haitians in Quebec shouldn't be minimized. But he understood it too late. My brother-in-law, last month, drove Trudeau. Trudeau is a trickster. You can never tell what he's thinking."

"If you're so powerful, why don't you work in management positions instead of driving taxis?"

"Those who really have power should never let themselves be seen. You saw the Italian community. They showed too much strength, and today you never hear about them. But . . ."

"But what?"

"We're in danger right now. If we let them do it, the Quebeckers will take this country from us."

"You just told me that real power should never show its face."

"This is different. Action is needed. Take my card. Call me. We have a meeting tonight in the basement of the Notre-Dame church."

Here's the big difference between Haitians and Quebeckers. Quebeckers think about politics solely in terms of independence, while Haitians think only of power. Each Haitian taxi driver firmly believes that if he really wanted to, he could become premier of Quebec while waiting to become president of Haiti. Having the power in Quebec is only a pastime for the boring days of exile.

17. I learned to cook quickly enough. It's a good way to catch girls: a good spicy Creole dish, an old bottle of Haitian rum (Barbancourt is the best Caribbean rum, according to Haitian nationalists, myself included), Tabou Combo (my favourite

group at the time). Everything went very well. We ate well, we drank, we danced and we made love. Perfect plan. We fell asleep in each other's arms.

All of a sudden she shakes me sharply. I wake up with a start.

"What's going on?"

"I don't understand," she says, a little frightened. "You were fighting with someone in your dream."

"What was I saying?"

"I don't know. You were speaking Creole. You were yelling, fighting, it scared me—but I'm sorry for having woken you up."

I know very well what's going on, but how to tell this comparative literature student that I was dreaming about werewolves? They were trying to get me once again, and like all the previous nights (it's why I rarely ask girls to stay the night) I had to fight to keep them from carrying me off. But how do I explain that to this young North American? The devils from my country never leave me. As soon as the lights are out, like cockroaches, they gather around my bed. To be afraid of devils at my age is equivalent, here, to an adult who wets his bed. Full of shame, I decide to scare her.

"It's you I was defending, you know."

"Oh, good," she says, vaguely worried.

"The thing is, I'm married to a very jealous voodoo goddess, so when there's a woman in my bed, she sees red." Voodoo, I know, works every time.

"And . . ."

"Well, I have to fight so that she won't hurt the woman."

A long silence.

"I have an exam this morning, I have to go review my notes," she says suddenly. "I'm sorry. . . . We'll see each other tomorrow night."

I let her go, knowing she'll never come back. I had a choice between giving myself the reputation of a ridiculous seducer who still dreams of devils or passing as the husband of a jealous voodoo goddess. I'm sure there are still those reckless enough to want to dethrone the blood-thirsty goddess Erzulie Dantor.

I don't know why we continue to have such nightmares. Our demons follow us. Dreams play an important role in the life of every human being, but even more in the life of someone uprooted. Each night, he does the journey back. It's the only way to escape from the madness. At the same time, he needs to get rid of his devils if he hopes to embrace the present. North American life takes place by day, not by night. All conquest is done during the day. Night is for rest, desire and alcohol. The newly arrived immigrant must confront the Western machine by day, and at night, the tropical devils. Finally, he's an exhausted man.

18. People from the north believe that winter, especially snow, is the main event of the journey. It's true that it's a big part of it. But it's the move on the social ladder that fascinates me. You go abruptly from the enviable status of intellectual middle class in Haiti to that of worker. And it's not a summer job like for young North American students.

The first day I found myself in front of a machine, it took me a long moment to understand what was happening to me. In Haiti, the economic situation might have been disastrous, but I had a social status. My father was a journalist, very briefly the mayor of Port-au-Prince, Assistant-Secretary of State and finally diplomat. My mother was an archivist. My grandparents lived comfortably in Petit Goâve. And there I was in front of a machine designed to crush me (I almost lost an arm the first day), in front of all these people who believed it was the best thing that could happen to me. To them, my condition had never been better. I spent the afternoon in the factory washrooms thinking about my new condition. I was a worker, an immigrant and a black. Bingo! The bottom of the barrel.

I went home. I was totally down. I sat in the middle of the room, in the dark. For the first time in my life I wasn't thinking about a political, literary or philosophical problem, but about what was happening to me in everyday life. *Real life,* as they say in Quebec. The question wasn't what I would become, but rather what I planned to do with myself. For the first time my life was in my own hands. It was both terrifying and exciting.

I was alone in this city, the trunk of the genealogical tree—nobody before me, and no descendants yet. I was no longer the son here, but not yet a father. Only me. The tree would bend in the direction I gave it. The new Quebec friends I spent my evenings with in the bars came mostly from those spruce little suburban cities surrounding Montreal. They didn't in fact travel too far from the family nest. From time to time, when things were going badly for them, they wouldn't be seen for one or two weeks, and we would learn that they had gone to recuperate at the family home (in Repentigny, Sainte-Thérèse, Saint-Marc or Joliette). As for me, there was nobody behind me. Without a net. And it's what saved me.

19. If I had left one culture, it wasn't to throw myself into a new one. Wandering. *Wanderooting*, as my friend Jean-Claude Charles says. The best way to get to know a city is to constantly change neighbourhoods. A new metro station to discover, new faces. I remember the endless nights spent talking at La Scala. There I discovered dancers, photographers, musicians and poets. This night crowd contrasted well with the young workers with whom I spent my days. The workers talked of nothing but women, sex and hockey, and always in very vulgar terms. And at night I found these gentle dreamers, starving philosophers, dazzled musicians. I was trying as much as possible to reconcile these two parallel worlds. I made myself invisible. I observed. And someone, one night, turned towards me.

"And you, what do you do?"

"What?"

"What do you do in life?"

A pause. The whole table is watching me now. It is the first time they have really seen me.

I have to say that I almost never speak during these meetings.

"You must do something," says someone else in a more friendly tone.

"I'm writing a novel," I finally answer.

General surprise. They are writing short stories, poems, tales, but nobody in the group is writing a novel.

"And what's it about?"

Again silence.

"We shouldn't bother him," says a girl. "Some writers don't like to talk about the book they're working on. You see, I've known him a long time now and I didn't know he was a writer."

"I'm not a writer. I'm writing a novel, that's all."

From that moment on, they saw me differently. My silence gained a certain weight. I had a precise function in the group. Sometimes, in the middle of a conversation, someone would say: "Be careful, guys, the writer is taking down everything you say."

This was how I started writing down my friends' conversations. To get myself into the atmosphere, I went to La Scala right after work. In the afternoon, it's a traditional Greek bar with old Greeks telling each other stories about Greece.

There were a dozen of them who bothered the waitress while eating souvlaki and overly sweet desserts. I sat in a corner, beside the window. And I wrote. Anything. Bits of conversation from the night before. Little stories of seduction that happened here at night. The story of that magnificent waitress we were all more or less in love with. She wasn't really interested in anyone, but she was always nice to everybody. All the more inaccessible. Like Mount Everest.

One night, a guy came in. He sat a little out of the way. And I saw her go crazy. She never stopped walking around him. Even so, you could tell she was trying to resist. She was doing what she could to avoid his corner. But she was helpless. The attraction was too strong. And she finally started to go over under more and more wacky pretexts. I was, I think, the only one to observe this game. There she was coming out of the washroom, and out of the corner of my eye I could see her wan face. The lightning had just struck her. She passed in front of me (as though a zombie) to go sit in front of the guy.

I could capture about ten stories like this in just one night (not all with this intensity). Separations. Reconciliations. Tender feelings. And the next day, I would write all this down in my notebook. Some time later, I would forget the names, the faces, to remember only the situations. It's chaos, therefore a novel.

20. I had a Senegalese friend who always came home at the beginning of spring. Nobody knew where he spent the winters. Winter is a time of profound privacy. People born here usually know how to face it, and there are even those who like it. Those who hate it make off for the south. I can't imagine the south (where it's warm) as a vacation place. I would lose any sense of origin. I come from the south. The south could never be synonymous with pleasure for me. The south doesn't sing in my head—solemn place. The cold terrorizes me.

I found out by chance that my friend generally spent the winter in a psychiatric hospital. He would regularly stand nude in the middle of the snow, and the police would come to collect him. He pretended to be a tree. The man was a walking tree without leaves. He never said a word about his stays in the hospital.

Another friend, this one Haitian, spends the winter in prison, in Waterloo. It seems they treat people well there. He found this out by accident. He was arrested one day because of unpaid parking tickets. And in prison, a big bearded man explained to him that there's this magnificent little prison where he was in the habit of spending the winter without being bothered too much. Don't have to pay anything. On government money. One day, when my friend was broke, he tried (don't ask me what you do to get in; I didn't know you could choose your prison), and since then he spends winters there, reading Dostoyevsky. He's crazy for Dosto.

When you live in the city and you don't have a chalet in the Laurentians, the only places really favourable for rest and reflection are prisons and hospitals. You still have to find a good one, though, like Waterloo.

21. I don't know exactly when I forgot the taste of sapodilla. Even in Haiti, you find them less and less. I remember that trip across the country with the writer Jean-Claude Charles, based in Paris. Just after Jean-Claude Duvalier left Haiti. We were searching feverishly for a sapodilla. The taste of that fruit literally haunted me. Charles found my obsession funny, but he took it seriously. Every individual searches for a lost smell or taste from his emotional environment. For me, it's sapodilla.

We asked at each place we passed if there was

a sapodilla tree. The peasants smiled, shaking their heads no. Without the taste of sapodilla, I had the impression that Haiti was noticeably moving away from me. The irony is that sapodilla didn't especially interest me when I lived in Haiti. Just like that, any time anywhere, a taste (or rather the nostalgia for a taste) can suddenly rise up from the depths of childhood.

22. I still remember that, during that trip, I never stopped dreaming of Montreal, which had never happened to me throughout my whole stay in Montreal. When I was in Montreal by day, it was Port-au-Prince that occupied my nights. When I'm in Port-au-Prince, it's Montreal that occupies my nights. Today, I'm in Miami, but I've never dreamed of this city. Instead, I have a rather strange dream: I see myself in Montreal, on Saint-Denis Street, but the colours and smells are still those of Port-au-Prince. When I'm in a city, I live in it; when I'm no longer there, it's the city that lives in me.

Translated from the French by LEXique Ltd.

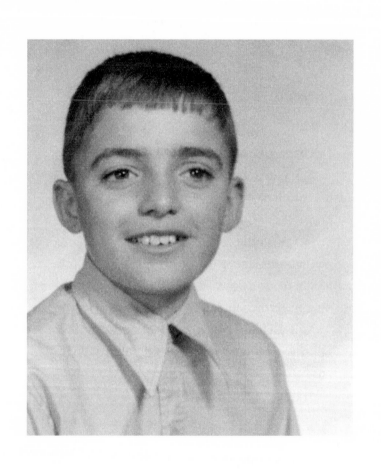

$\mathscr{Nino}$ **Ricci**

A PASSAGE TO CANADA

WHILE MY OWN ENTRY into Canada was by that most traumatic of emigrations, birth, my parents, who arrived here a few years ahead of me, in 1954, apparently had a much easier time of it, cruising into Halifax's Pier 21 aboard the well-appointed passenger liner *Saturnia*. To hear them tell it, they had the time of their lives on the crossing, dining and dancing and living it up, giving the lie to those images we were all raised on of the poor immigrant masses stumbling out of the darkened holds of rat-infested, cholera-infected death ships. By the 1950s, it seems, the days of lightless steerage berths and of fatal island quarantines had passed, and for about three hundred dollars—roughly what you could save in a year—any two-bit peasant or labourer could book a fairly comfortable passage to the New World.

For my parents, that passage had its origins in my father's year of army service, when, stationed in northern Italy far from the mountains of his native

Molise, he gazed for the first time on the beautiful flat green fields of the Po Valley. The sight made him wonder why he and his family had been wasting their time on the few craggy acres of hillside they scrabbled a living from back home; it seems it had never occurred to him before then that elsewhere things might be different. Not long afterwards the chance arose to come to Canada, and he was quick to take it. The flat fields that greeted his arrival here, however, were a far cry from those of the Po: windswept and snow-covered and bleak, they seemed the last outreaches of the habitable world. Coming from Italy, where even the dog houses had walls of foot-thick stone, he and my mother were made somewhat concerned by the rickety wooden shacks that seemed to form the primary residences here, and by the tiny, even more rickety ones out back that they feared might be the workers' quarters, though one whiff of them would quickly have explained their function.

As it happened, my parents' first home in Canada, in the small farming town of Leamington, Ontario, was not so far removed from those rickety outhouses: set off the barn of a farmer who had sponsored them for their first year of work here, it was essentially a refurbished chicken coop. A couple of my brothers were born there, and afterwards my parents remembered the place fondly enough; and indeed an uncle of mine, Luigi, subsequently took it over, and stayed on for the next thirty years working at the local Heinz factory and living the bachelor life before finally returning to Italy to the wife and son he'd left behind there. We used to visit him sometimes Sunday mornings after mass and he always seemed so settled and self-sufficient and in his element in that elfin habitation, with his army-sized cot and his stoop-shouldered Kelvinator fridge and the little shot glasses he'd bring out for a glass of Tia Maria or anisette. It was a kind of shock to me as I grew older to learn that he had this completely other life across the sea that he would be returning to, and that everything here—his blackened espresso pot, his tiny sloped-ceilinged rooms—was merely provisional, a way station. I had not quite understood then this dual-sidedness of immigration, how there was always an absent reference point that the present stood against, and that could make the present's nuts-and-bolts everydayness and permanence suddenly appear the merest shadow.

By the time I was born—the fifth of seven children, though one, a girl, had died as an infant back in Italy—my parents had purchased a small farm and our household had burgeoned to include a set of grandparents and my father's two unmarried sisters. In some important respects, the world I arrived into was not so different from the one my parents had left behind: the language we spoke was the dialect my parents had brought with them; the festivals we cele-brated were the local ones of their hometowns; the people we saw were my parents' siblings and cousins and neighbours from back home. My mother's home-town of Villa Canale, which had a population of about a thousand just after the war, eventually, in a kind of mitosis, lost some half of these to Leamington; and so it might have been true to claim that those who left ended up no less at home than those who stayed behind. Indeed, I often heard it said that fellow villagers got along much better in Canada than they ever had in their hometowns, where they'd had centuries of feuds and old land disputes and the like to divide them, and where everyone had been careful not to let their neighbours know their busi-ness. In Canada, on the other hand, at planting time, every *paesan* and third cousin from back home would show up in your field to help you out. Some of my best memories from early childhood are of those days in the fields, the jugs of Kool-Aid I'd lug around to people while they worked and the mid-morning breaks we'd take with coffee and biscuits and slabs of cheese and salted pork passed around on the tip of someone's jackknife.

Often enough the cheese and pork would be of our own vintage; we used to hang them to cure from the rafters of our barn, with shields fashioned from Unico Vegetable Oil tins positioned above them to keep off the pigeon droppings. The pork came from the hog that we slaughtered every year in mid-winter: it would show up in our basement one day grunting and heaving, live and primal and real, and be sausage and tripe by the following night. This yearly slaughter, which had always to be during the waxing moon or the meat would go bad, was accompanied by a party, for which the relatives were invited over and sheets of plywood were laid on sawhorses in the living room for tables, the windows fogging up with the heat of cooking and talk. All of these things, of course—the pigs in the basement, the parties, even the Unico tins in the barn—seemed perfectly normal and inevitable to me when I was small, not because they recalled customs my parents had had in Italy, which in any event I knew nothing of, but simply because, not unlike my father back in Molise, I had never realized that elsewhere things might be different.

When I started school, however, a lot of what we did suddenly began to seem not so normal. There was

the homemade bread my mother used for our sandwiches, thick-crusted, spongy stuff that she'd fashioned baking pans for from those same all-purpose
Unico tins and that did not resemble in the least the
white, perfect, store-bought bread of the other kids;
there was the patched, old-fashioned, hand-me-down
look of our clothes. It was as if I too had set out on a
ship and arrived in another country, where people did
things differently, so that suddenly everything about
my own little domain, the closed autonomous world I'd
been raised in until then, seemed makeshift and shabby
and low. This, then, perhaps, was my true passage to
Canada, out of innocence and sameness into difference, and like any child, I did not like the experience of
difference one bit, and sought every means to mitigate
it. Thus all things Italian became anathema, and the
two worlds I lived in, at home and at school, were kept
cleanly separate and distinct, so that the former should
not in any way compromise my standing in the latter.
In this way I sailed more or less happily towards assimilation, which seemed the good and proper course for
someone of my clearly questionable origins.

In the summer of 1971, I made my first visit to Italy,
as part of a family trip that lasted six weeks and took

us to every corner of the country. That trip transformed my relationship to my parents' homeland: from an Italianness that had meant shabby clothes and spongy bread, I discovered one that included instead such marvels as the Colosseum and Saint Mark's Square, which even the callow twelve-year-old I was then could not help but be impressed by. Indeed, Italy, in its excess, seemed precisely designed for twelve-year-olds, since every sort of wonder could be found there, from skeleton-filled catacombs to vast marble monuments and endless miles of sand-brimmed sea; and I immediately fell hopelessly in love with the place, with exactly that achy, adolescent intensity I had begun to feel by then towards the opposite sex. The Italy I fell in love with, however, was not the one my parents had left behind. In fact, in most of the places we visited they were as much tourists as I was, and were laying eyes on them for the first time. Thus what we were discovering together was precisely the Italy that my parents had always been excluded from, coming as they had from the barbarous south, where feudalism hadn't been abolished until the 1850s and where Mussolini, who had been the first to introduce there such extravagances as hospitals and schools, was still considered a hero.

It was a bit of a shock to me, then, to arrive at this other Italy, that of my parents' little mountain villages, and to find there an entirely different world, of abandoned houses and questionable plumbing and animal shit in the roads. What in the rest of Italy had seemed venerable and ancient here seemed merely backward, and my first reaction was a wish to flee back to the elegant apartment blocks and terraced inner courtyards of my sophisticated Roman cousins. I remember the supper we had our first evening in my grandfather's house in Villa Canale, the flies everywhere and the stable stink from outside, the gobs of spit on the hearth where my grandfather had hawked towards the cooking fire and missed. We had penne with tomato sauce for supper, but I could not eat a bite of them, so much did the place turn my stomach. Seeing the bathroom, a crude addition to the place from the early sixties, when indoor plumbing had apparently still been a great novelty, I was relieved to learn that one of my uncles had recently built a new home down the street with somewhat more updated facilities, including the luxury of a water heater and a bathtub.

I cannot call up now what I had thought my parents' birthplace would actually be like, based on the mythologizing anecdotes and commentaries I'd heard from them until then. But surely I had not imagined it as anything quite so unsettling and strange, so real, as what actually confronted me. There was so much texture to the place, so much taste and sight and smell, that it seemed an affront—the hot days and cold nights, the smell of animals and smoke, the dwarfish aunts with rotted teeth and the grandmother who did not rise the long day from her chair and who did not speak, so that the flies made a home in the folds of her copious overgarments and shawls and I could not have told if she was living or dead. Every morning my mother used to send me across town to buy a jug of milk from a woman who kept a cow there, which now, of course, conjures up images of the pure peasant wholesomeness of things fresh from the source; but at the time, fetching that milk still frothy and warm from the cow like that, in a stable that smelled like one and that was thick with those ubiquitous flies, I could hardly bring myself to drink the stuff.

What I had thus discovered was that at age twelve I was already well confirmed in my bias towards such modern values as hygiene and pasteurization and hot baths, and did not find it pleasant to be deprived of them. I counted it as hopeless backward-ness, for instance—even though later I remembered these things as the mark of a great quaintness and charm—that Villa Canale boasted at the time only a single telephone, at the local bar and general store, and a single TV, which the owner would kindly set out on his balcony above the village square every evening for communal viewing. Back then I thought of this side of myself, the one that felt horrified at the prospect of several weeks without the familiar trappings of modern living, as my Canadian side, since at home I had always taken such things as hot water and TVs utterly for granted. But in fact this love of amenity was rather more universal than that. Italy itself, after all, was no stranger to modernity: it was there, in the bathroom of an expressway service station, that three decades ago I first came across what has only in recent years become standard issue in Canada, the automatic water faucet. So while I thought that my parents' villages had helped make me aware of that part of me that was irreducibly Canadian—ironically, just at the point when I was learning to love my Italianness—what they really did was uncover in me more or less the same instinct that had led my parents to emigrate, namely, the desire for a more comfortable life. Perhaps my parents could not have named so precisely what it was they were after, the exact kitchen appliance or brand of TV; and yet it was the general siren call of such things, of the whole luxurious modern world, that drew them away, and that even still meant that the young in these villages left for the cities the minute they were able. It should not have been a surprise to me, then, how in Canada the new homes of Italians, fitted with every modern convenience, became their symbols of success, and how within them the bathrooms in particular represented a special apotheosis, so much so that there was usually one bathroom, complete with every fixture and frill and decked out in the finest Italian marble, that was absolutely off limits except to special visitors, and stood as a kind of shrine to having arrived.

Back in Villa Canale, however, a strange thing had begun to happen to me: with each day that passed, the place got more and more under my skin, not so much that I could have said I was actually growing to like it, but certainly so that I could not ignore it. For instance there was a boy that I met there, Peppino, twelve like me, who, however, smoked and drank and walked around in a man's corduroy cap and suspenders, and who knew one word of English, *fock,* which he gave me to believe he understood something of from first-hand experience. He led me up to his uncle's place once and we sat in the cellar there drinking wine together, which his uncle poured off for us as if it were nothing unusual for a couple of twelve-year-olds to stop in of an afternoon for a taste of his latest vintage. I do not remember much of the rest of that day except how much stranger still Villa Canale seemed to me when it was spinning around at great speed, and when even the cobblestones beneath my feet could not keep from shifting and seething with each step. Then there were my cousins, my father's nieces, who lived just beyond my father's hometown of Poggio Sannita in the Valley of the Pigs: four girls who ranged in age from eleven to eighteen, and all of whom made my breath go short with their sheer earthy loveliness and perfection. The eldest, Marisa, would walk with me arm in arm sometimes through the pastures and promise to marry me, and it was all I could do then not to keep my heart from bursting from the wish that such a hopeless thing were possible.

It was also in this time that I finally met Uncle Luigi's wife, my mother's sister Maria. Small and bright-eyed and bluntly, unceremoniously generous and open-handed, she seemed not so much a good match for Uncle Luigi as literally his other half, living out for him here that portion of his life he had left behind. The house she lived in had been built with the money he had sent over from Canada, complete with a winery and cold house out back; but he himself had yet to lay eyes on it. For my own part, I felt as if I were looking inside Uncle Luigi's head, seeing there his dream of return, that part of him that was always elsewhere.

Indeed, the entire village had this sense to it of somehow doubling over all my experience in Canada, since I could not step from my grandfather's door without seeing some face that was the exact duplicate of one back home or some way of doing things that mirrored our own, as if everyone who had gone had left behind here this secret other life that had continued unabated after they had set out. I might have said that they'd left here the ghosts of themselves, and of their former lives, had it not rather begun to seem by then that this was the life that was visceral and real and the one in Canada the ghostly one, merely this one's pale imitation. It seemed a strange kind of haunting, these two worlds so distant and complete in themselves and yet each of which seemed the other's shadow, as if I might round a corner and what was strange would suddenly become familiar as day, and it would be time to slaughter the pig and set out the sawhorses or to bring the bread and cheese to the fields for the morning merenda.

Years later, when I came to write my first novel, I was somewhat surprised to find myself going back for my material to that first visit to my parents' villages. Apparently they had lodged themselves much more deeply in my psyche than I had imagined; and the story they eventually gave rise to came upon me practically unawares, so that characters and settings and scenes sprang out of me almost fully formed, as if they had simply been awaiting the moment that I would set them free. Curiously, there was almost nothing in the novel of the tourist's Italy I had been so enamoured of as a child, and that indeed I had continued to love; rather it was the world of stables and flies that my imagination had been fired by, as if the more sophisticated Italy of monuments and automatic water faucets had been merely the back door for my entry into my own proper Italy, the one my beautiful cousins lived in and my diminutive, no-nonsense aunts. That first novel ended with a sea journey aboard a ship called *Saturnia;* and now, in retrospect, it almost seems to me that my real passage to Canada came exactly in that fictive voyage, at the point when I was finally able to fully imagine the place I needed to set out from, since without a point of departure there could be no arrival.

Towards the end of my stay in Villa Canale I took a walk with my sister one day down to the river that wound its way through the valley that the village overlooked. The trip was much longer than we had judged, down steep, winding goat paths that passed through vineyards and wheat fields and rocky pasture; and once we had arrived and had wandered for a ways along the river, we looked around us and suddenly realized we were hopelessly, utterly lost, some shift in the landscape having erased every landmark that might have pointed us back to Villa Canale. We finally stumbled upon a crooked byroad that looked as if it might lead in the proper direction and started up it, beneath a relentless mid-afternoon sun; but each twist in the road seemed only to further disorient us, and take us into increasing eeriness and unfamiliarity. We passed tiny villages where dogs barked furiously from courtyards but not a soul stirred; we heard the cicadas screech at us from the roadside weeds; we saw a snake slither across our path and into a gully. Our legs by then were beyond tired, but we dared not stop for fear we could not continue again. Our throats were beyond parched, but there was not a fountain to be seen, and the one hole-in-the-wall village shop we eventually passed was boarded up for the afternoon closing. And so we trudged on, ready to perish there in the Molisan wilderness, two hapless *americani* who had foolishly wandered too far from home.

Then suddenly we crested a hill and found ourselves on the high road into Villa Canale. A young woman of the village, one of several I had worshipped from afar, was just coming in from the fields and instantly recognized us.

"You've been to the river," she said, and it was all I could do to nod agreement, so relieved was I to see a familiar face.

"You want to be careful down there," she said. "They're not civilized like we are up here in the hills."

Then she took my arm in hers and led us back into Villa Canale, and we passed the cellar where I'd got drunk, the post office and the bar, the balcony where the TV was set out every night, and the village seemed no longer a foreign place I was visiting but a familiar one I was returning to. In fact it had always been, but I hadn't seen that, the shadow at the back of our lives that had always dogged us, now finally brought to the light of day.

Acknowledgements

The Dominion Institute would like to thank an outstanding group of civic-minded individuals and organizations for facilitating the publication of this book. Initial funding for *Passages to Canada* was provided by the Ministry of Citizenship and Immigration Canada. Westwood Creative Artists was instrumental in bringing together a phenomenal group of authors to contribute their stories. Richard Addis and Simon Beck of *The Globe and Mail* were responsible for printing the first iteration of this collection. And finally, thanks to Doubleday Canada and Maya Mavjee, who expertly saw this book through to publication.

For more information on the Passages to Canada project including free, bilingual teaching resources, visit www.passagestocanada.com.

Notes on Contributors

MICHELLE BERRY was born in San Francisco, California, and was raised in Victoria, British Columbia. She is the author of two collections of short stories, *How to Get There From Here* (1997) and *Margaret Lives in the Basement* (1998), and two novels, *What We All Want* (2001) and *Blur* (2002). Along with Natalee Caple, Berry co-edited the anthology, *The Notebooks: Interviews and New Fiction from Contemporary Writers*. In addition to her writing, she teaches at Ryerson University, reviews for *The Globe and Mail*, and served for four years on the board of PEN Canada.

YING CHEN was born in Shanghai and emigrated to Montreal in 1989. She has published four major works in French, *Memory of Water* (1992), *Chinese Letters* (1993), *Ingratitude* (1995), and *Immobile* (1998). *Ingratitude* was nominated for the Governor General's Award and the Prix Femina, and received the Quebec-Paris prize, as well as the Grand Reader's Prize from *Elle Quebec*. It has been translated into English, Spanish, Italian, and Polish.

RUDYARD GRIFFITHS is a founding member and the executive director of the Dominion Institute, a national charity dedicated to the promotion of Canadian history and civics. He has written extensively on the themes of Canadian history, identity and cultures for *The Globe and Mail*, *The National Post* and *Maclean's*. *Passages* is the second book the Dominion Institute has published with Doubleday Canada. It follows *Story of a Nation* (2001).

MICHAEL IGNATIEFF is the director of the Carr Center for Human Rights Policy at Harvard University. Concerned with ethnic war, he has travelled to Serbia, Croatia, Bosnia, Rwanda, and Afghanistan, and has written extensively on ethnic war and the unique responsibilities it imposes. His non-academic work includes *The Russian Album, A Family Memoir*, which won the Governor General's Award and the Heinemann Prize of Britain's Royal Society of Literature in 1988, and *Scar Tissue*, which was short-listed for the Booker Prize in 1993.

BRIAN D. JOHNSON is an award-winning journalist who serves as senior entertainment writer and film critic at *Maclean's* magazine. His non-fiction books include *Brave Films, Wild Nights: 25 Years of Festival Fever*. He has also published a novel, *Volcano Days*, and a book of poetry, *Marzipan Lies*. He lives in Toronto with his wife, Marni, and their son, Casey.

DANY LAFERRIÈRE was born in the village of Petit Goave, Haiti. He wrote for *Le Petit Samedi Soir* and worked for Radio-Haiti International until he was forced to emigrate to Quebec in the late 1970s. He has published a number of novels, among them: *How to Make Love to a Negro Without Getting Tired* (1987), *An Aroma of Coffee* (1993), *Dining With the Dictator* (1994), and *A Drifting Year* (1997). He has received many prizes for his writing, notably the Carbet de la Caribe Prize, and the Edgar-Lesperance Prize.

ALBERTO MANGUEL was born in Buenos Aires, and worked in publishing in Italy, France, England, and Tahiti before arriving in Canada in the early 1980s. Manguel began his distinguished career with the first edition of *The Dictionary of Imaginary Places* (1980). *A History of Reading* was published in 1998, and was awarded France's prestigious Prix Médicis. Manguel is also the author of *Reading Pictures* (2000). He is recognized as an accomplished editor, translator, anthologist, essayist, and novelist.

ANNA PORTER was born in Hungary. Her family settled in New Zealand after the 1956 Revolution. She began her publishing career in England, then moved to Canada in 1968. Anna Porter is publisher of Key Porter Books, and is one of Canada's most resected publishing professionals. She is the author of three crime novels: *Hidden Agenda*, *Mortal Sins*, and *The Bookfair Murders*, which was made into a movie. Her most recent book, *The Storyteller: Memory, Secrets, Magic and Lies*, is a non-fiction account of the story of Hungary and of Porter's family. An Officer of the Order of Canada, Anna Porter lives in Toronto with her husband and two daughters.

NINO RICCI was born near Leamington, Ontario, to parents who had only recently emigrated from Italy. His *Lives of the Saints* (1990) won the Governor General's Award for Fiction, the SmithBooks/ Books in Canada First Novel Award, and the F.G. Bressani Prize. The novel was also a national bestseller, and was followed by the highly acclaimed *In a Glass House* (1993) and *Where She Has Gone* (1997), which was a finalist for the Giller Prize. Nino Ricci lives in Toronto. His most recent novel is *Testament*.

SHYAM SELVADURAI was born in Colombo, Sri Lanka. His family moved to Canada in 1983. Sevadurai's first novel, *Funny Boy*, was published in 1994 and received the W.H. Smith/ Books in Canada First Novel Award. His second novel, *Cinnamon Gardens*, was published in 1998. He lives in Toronto.

M.G. VASSANJI was born in Kenya and raised in Tanzania. Before coming to Canada in 1978, he attended M.I.T., and later was writer in residence at the University of Iowa. Vassanji is the author of four acclaimed novels: *The Gunny Sack* (1989), which won a regional Commonwealth Prize; *No New Land* (1991); *The Book of Secrets* (1994), which won The Giller Prize; and *Amriika* (1999). He was awarded the Harbourfront Festival Prize in 1994 in recognition of his achievement in and contribution to the world of letters, and was in the same year chosen as one of twelve Canadians on *Maclean's* Honour Roll.

KEN WIWA is the son of murdered Nigerian writer, journalist, and human rights activist, Ken Saro-Wiwa. During his father's incarceration and trial, Ken Wiwa travelled the world, tirelessly lobbying world leaders, writing, speaking, and campaigning for his father and the Ogoni people. His memoir, *In the Shadow of a Saint* (2000), chronicles these experiences. Ken Wiwa moved to Toronto with his wife and son in May 1999. He is a former journalist and editor at *The Guardian*, writes for *The Globe and Mail*, and is a senior resident writer at Massey College, University of Toronto.

MOSES ZNAIMER was born in the former Soviet republic of Tajikistan during WW II. His family, having been driven from their homes by the advancing German armies, finally fled to Canada in 1948 from Stalin's consolidation of the Soviet empire. Znaimer is co-founder, president and executive producer of Citytv, and is the creative force behind more than a dozen CHUM Television Specialty Channels including: MuchMusic, MuchMoreMusic, MusiquePlus, MusiMax, Bravo!, Space, CablePulse24, Canadian Learning Television, Star!, FashionTelevision, BookTelevision, Sextv, and CourtTV Canada.